Mapping with Drupal

Alan Palazzolo and Thomas Turnbull

Beijing · Cambridge · Farnham · Köln · Sebastopol · Tokyo

Mapping with Drupal
by Alan Palazzolo and Thomas Turnbull

Published by O'Reilly Media, Inc., 1005 Gravenstein Highway North, Sebastopol, CA 95472.

O'Reilly books may be purchased for educational, business, or sales promotional use. Online editions are also available for most titles (*http://my.safaribooksonline.com*). For more information, contact our corporate/institutional sales department: (800) 998-9938 or *corporate@oreilly.com*.

Editor: Julie Steele
Production Editor: Teresa Elsey

Cover Designer: Karen Montgomery
Interior Designer: David Futato
Illustrator: Robert Romano

Revision History for the First Edition:
   2011-12-15   First release
See *http://oreilly.com/catalog/errata.csp?isbn=9781449308940* for release details.

ISBN: 978-1-449-30894-0

[LSI]

1323958752

Table of Contents

Preface

Audience

This book is intended for people building Drupal websites who would like to visualize their content on a map. Maps are powerful and can tell a rich story. A map is instantly readable, but at the same time almost infinitely revealing. With the rise of maps on the Internet and now on cell phones, the way we navigate our lives has changed. Recognizing this, more web developers are integrating location into websites and applications.

Drupal is a versatile content management system, and because of that, it has been extended through many contributed modules to support mapping. Drupal is not primarily a mapping platform, however, so mapping in Drupal can be tricky. But because Drupal is so extendable, mapping in Drupal can be adapted to your specific needs. This book will help you navigate these complexities to create beautiful and engaging maps.

By the end of this book, you will be able to create a website with a map that automatically centers on the user's location. The map will include events and local groups that have been added through intuitive interfaces. Rather than using one of the maps from Google or Bing that have become so familiar, perhaps you will create a custom base map that fits the color scheme of your site. And rather than some pink pins, the events and local groups shown on your map will be marked with custom icons created for your site.

We assume you know how to install Drupal, install contributed modules, and enable themes; maybe you have already built a site that is used publicly. If you have not done these things or feel you do not have a great grasp on Drupal, don't stop reading this book just yet. Read over the first few chapters to get a feel for what is possible, take that enthusiasm and read over some other tutorials or books to learn the basics of site building with Drupal, and then come back. There are some great titles to get you started working with Drupal, some of which are listed in Appendix A. But don't worry, we will try our best to not assume too much.

Later in this book, we will look at writing code to extend existing mapping modules. When we get there, we will assume you know a little about writing Drupal modules;

at a minimum you should understand how to create a simple custom module for a site and be familiar with Drupal hooks. If you are new to writing Drupal modules, there are some books listed in Appendix A that will help you get up to speed developing for Drupal.

Drupal and Mapping Glossary

Drupal and web mapping come with specific terminology that is helpful when talking about these technologies, like *modules*, *nodes*, *map tiles*, and *WKT*. If you are new to Drupal or web mapping and these terms are not familiar, take a moment to read Appendix C now. We will also be explaining some of these terms throughout the book, particularly in Chapter 2.

Drupal 7 Modules

This book is written for Drupal 7, which was released in January 2011. Most of what we shall discuss will use contributed modules found on *http://drupal.org*. As we write this book, most of the modules mentioned are in active development, and they may or may not have full releases specifically for Drupal 7. Though we are confident that the ideas and structures will remain consistent, interfaces and module versions may change a bit from what you read in this book. We will do our best to keep this publication up to date as this dynamic topic changes. Errata will be listed at the URL in "How to Contact Us" on page x.

Conventions Used in This Book

The following typographical conventions are used in this book:

Italic
> Indicates new terms, URLs, email addresses, filenames, and file extensions.

`Constant width`
> Used for program listings, as well as within paragraphs to refer to program elements such as variable or function names, databases, data types, environment variables, statements, and keywords.

`Constant width bold`
> Shows commands or other text that should be typed literally by the user.

`Constant width italic`
> Shows text that should be replaced with user-supplied values or by values determined by context.

This icon signifies a tip, suggestion, or general note.

 This icon indicates a warning or caution.

Using Code Examples

This book is here to help you get your job done. In general, you may use the code in this book in your programs and documentation. You do not need to contact us for permission unless you're reproducing a significant portion of the code. For example, writing a program that uses several chunks of code from this book does not require permission. Selling or distributing a CD-ROM of examples from O'Reilly books does require permission. Answering a question by citing this book and quoting example code does not require permission. Incorporating a significant amount of example code from this book into your product's documentation does require permission.

We appreciate, but do not require, attribution. An attribution usually includes the title, author, publisher, and ISBN. For example: "*Mapping with Drupal* by Alan Palazzolo and Thomas Turnbull (O'Reilly). Copyright 2012 Alan Palazzolo and Thomas Turnbull, 978-1-449-30894-0."

If you feel your use of code examples falls outside fair use or the permission given above, feel free to contact us at *permissions@oreilly.com*.

Safari® Books Online

 Safari Books Online is an on-demand digital library that lets you easily search over 7,500 technology and creative reference books and videos to find the answers you need quickly.

With a subscription, you can read any page and watch any video from our library online. Read books on your cell phone and mobile devices. Access new titles before they are available for print, and get exclusive access to manuscripts in development and post feedback for the authors. Copy and paste code samples, organize your favorites, download chapters, bookmark key sections, create notes, print out pages, and benefit from tons of other time-saving features.

O'Reilly Media has uploaded this book to the Safari Books Online service. To have full digital access to this book and others on similar topics from O'Reilly and other publishers, sign up for free at *http://my.safaribooksonline.com*.

How to Contact Us

Please address comments and questions concerning this book to the publisher:

O'Reilly Media, Inc.
1005 Gravenstein Highway North
Sebastopol, CA 95472
800-998-9938 (in the United States or Canada)
707-829-0515 (international or local)
707-829-0104 (fax)

We have a web page for this book, where we list errata, examples, and any additional information. You can access this page at:

http://mappingdrupal.com

To comment or ask technical questions about this book, send email to:

bookquestions@oreilly.com

For more information about our books, courses, conferences, and news, see our website at *http://www.oreilly.com*.

Find us on Facebook: *http://facebook.com/oreilly*

Follow us on Twitter: *http://twitter.com/oreillymedia*

Watch us on YouTube: *http://www.youtube.com/oreillymedia*

Acknowledgments

Alan and Thomas would like to thank the book's technical reviewers, including Denis Wood, Sara Hodges, Robert Holmes, Joseph Bachana, Ronald Turnbull, Théodore Biadala, Reuben Turk, Ankur Rishi, and Patrick Hayes. Thanks also to Julie Steele from O'Reilly for guiding us through the writing process. And a very special thanks to all of the people who have contributed to Drupal and open source mapping over the years.

Alan has been working on the OpenLayers module for Drupal for almost three years and would like to thank all the amazing people that have helped out on the project and made it the successful project it is today. This includes all the committers, patch providers, documenters, and screencasters; thank you all very much. He would also like to thank the Drupal community as a whole for being so supportive and welcoming over the years; it is projects like Drupal that really show how open source is more than just code. He would also like to personally thank Ellie F. for supporting him through writing this book.

Thomas would like to thank his father, Ronald Turnbull, both for tirelessly editing the entire book and for teaching him as a five-year-old to read maps. He would also like to thank his geography teachers over the years, especially Irene McCann, George Dalling, and Bob Hodgart. Thanks go to Wendy Brawer at Green Map for introducing him to Drupal and the concept of open source mapmaking. Thanks finally to Sara Hodges for her input and support.

CHAPTER 1

Why Map with Drupal

Drupal powers over 1% of the Internet (*http://thinkdrop.net/blog/tue-05182010-1832/ case-you-didnt-hear-drupal-powers-1-web*), more than one million websites. Over a quarter of adult Americans use mobile or social location-based services such as Google Maps, Weather lookups, and restaurant searches (see Pew Internet (*http://pewinternet .org/Reports/2011/Location/Overview/Findings.aspx*)). As location becomes a core part of what users expect from websites and mobile devices, Drupal gives you the tools to create a website that meets these demands. Drupal's strength is in creating interactions between mapping data and all the other sorts of data (e.g., restaurant reviews, business locations, user locations, voting districts).

Chapters 1 and 2 focus on the theory of maps, cartography, and considerations of mapping in general. A well-designed and well-thought-out map can increase the usefulness and usability of a web application. At the same time, a cumbersome, badly devised map can frustrate users and drive them away from your site. These first two chapters will not instruct you in the technical abilities that you need to get maps on your Drupal site. Instead, and more importantly, they will help you think about the maps you are creating, what they are for, and what you expect the user to get out of them. If you just want to start making maps with Drupal, and you know exactly what maps you need, skip ahead to Chapter 3, but it is worth reading these introductory chapters and understanding your role as map maker.

Chapter 1 introduces mapping, specifically web mapping, and why you may want to make maps with Drupal. Chapter 2 dives deeper into the mapping concepts that you will come across, such as map projections and data storage, and outlines some of the challenges of making maps online. Chapters 3 and 4 contain an overview of the main mapping modules for Drupal and have detailed tutorials for configuring these modules to create maps. Chapter 3 focuses on the storage of spatial data and Chapter 4 covers using this data to create maps. Chapters 5 and 6 are about customizing the maps on your site by creating your own modules. Chapter 5 explains how to use JavaScript and PHP to add new ways of interacting with maps. Chapter 6 provides ways to make your maps look more beautiful. Chapter 7 pulls this all together with an explanation of how to configure your maps in code for use with version control.

The Power of Maps

Maps, generally defined, probably first appeared over 18,000 years ago (see Wikipedia (*http://en.wikipedia.org/wiki/History_of_cartography*)), but it wasn't really until the 1500s that maps (as we think of them today) were produced in large numbers (Woods, *Rethinking the Power of Maps*, page 27). Around that time, maps became significant navigational and military aids and powerful tools for cities, states, and nations to help organize boundaries and administrative activities. These maps started to outline and actually define states and other political boundaries. Woods writes, "the map possessed an all but unique power to give the elusive idea of the state concrete form, to those outside looking in, certainly, but also to those living within." This idea that maps have the power to literally define the world around us, and not just represent it, still holds true today and is in your hands as a map maker.

It is important to keep in mind that while maps are driven by data that has been collected, often from observed data, maps are not inherently objective artifacts. A common perception of a map is that it is a neutral display of collected data, similar to a spreadsheet. But there are many questions when looking at a spreadsheet or a map: How accurate is the data? How was the data collected? What data is not presented? These issues show the subjectivity of maps.

Maps are akin to statistics. This definition of statistics from Wikipedia (*http://en.wiki pedia.org/wiki/Statistics*) could apply to mapmaking: "Statistics is the study of the collection, organization, analysis, and interpretation of data." In statistics, data gets collected, aggregated, and then put through various mathematical algorithms to either prove or disprove a hypothesis, usually around some preexisting idea about the world. Statistics can easily be misused by applying specific methodologies to ensure a certain analytical outcome. In the same way, a mapmaker collects and combines a huge amount of data, simplifies and codifies it, and then presents it on paper or a computer screen so as to assert some specific idea. Depending on the decisions made throughout the process, that idea can be conveyed in many ways.

Maps are art. "Art is the product or process of deliberately arranging items (often with symbolic significance) in a way that influences and affects one or more of the senses, emotions, and intellect" (Wikipedia (*http://en.wikipedia.org/wiki/Art*)). Once data has been collected for a map, there are still many decisions to be made on how to visually communicate that data on a map, such as symbols, colors, interactions, or annotations. How does one symbolize a church? What color is a county road? Where will the legend be? With maps, as with art, every decision, no matter how small, is often intentional, so to convey a very specific vision to the viewer. In these decisions is the power to communicate with maps.

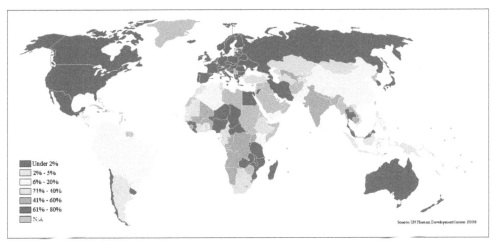

Figure 1-1. Percentage of population living on less than a dollar a day (2007–2008) from Wikipedia (http://en.wikipedia.org/wiki/File:Percentage_population_living_on_less_than_1_dollar _day_2007-2008.png)

Story Telling

Maps tell a story. Users expect a map to communicate an idea to them. This could be a story about how there are over a billion people that live on less than a dollar a day (see Figure 1-1). Or the story could be more complex, describing the rise, climax, and decline of newspapers in the United States over the past 300 years; this story was told in the interactive map by Standford's Rural West Initiative (*http://www.stanford.edu/ group/ruralwest/cgi-bin/drupal/visualizations/us_newspapers*).

With any kind of story telling, the more detailed and interactive you can be, the more likely you will be to keep your audience captivated. What colors should you use? What font should the street names be in? How should you use instructions and legends to teach people to interact with the map? What happens when a user clicks on a marker on the map? These decisions lead your users to the end of your story.

The Persuasion

> Through a cartographer's choices of selection, omission, or simplification, a map can be manipulated to illustrate entirely different human circumstances in the same physical geography.
>
> —John Brian Harley (*http://en.wikipedia.org/wiki/John_Brian_Harley*), map historian, 1989

Maps try to convince you that *something* is *somewhere*. The *something* could be physical like a tree or river, or it could be a territory, such as the State of California, or it could be a mere notion, like the idea that California is a Democratic state. The *somewhere* could be any place, but it is only useful if it is a place that we, as users, can connect ourselves to; it could be our town, our neighborhood, our country. Maps are also communicating to us by the things that are not somewhere on the map. These decisions assert an idea of what is important or what is not important, and collectively with the symbols, colors, lines, and dots that make a map, they create an argument for your user to agree with or not.

Most of what we see on maps we tend to believe without much thought, such as the national boundary of France, but other boundaries, such as the areas of Israel and Palestine, are currently disputed by many people, and maps help represent and define those positions. Maps are not wholly objective as discussed above. Maps can lie; even when no deceit is intended, the best mapping can, and often does, mislead for specific purposes. And even if what your map asserts may be trivial, by using map APIs such as Google or Bing map tiles, you are asserting all of the ideas and ideologies of that service as well as your own.

> All this is to say that mapmakers are not cognitive agents parachuted into a pre-given world with a chain and a theodolite, to measure and record what they find there. Rather, they're extraordinarily selective creators of a world—not *the* world, but *a* world—whose features they bring into being with a map. Mapmakers propose this, not that, observe these things, not those...
>
> —Denis Woods, *Rethinking the Power of Maps*, page 51

As a quick example, take a look at this map of California from 1940, which focuses on trying to convince the user that California an amazing place with lots of fun opportunities (Figure 1-2). This is in stark contrast to what a modern Google Maps Road Map of California does, focusing on providing road data and specific relevant features (Figure 1-3).

Conversations in Maps

In modern life, maps have become an almost instinctive way of seeing our world. In fact, they are our strongest, practically our only, way to perceive the world around us as a whole (given that most of us don't get to go on a space walk). Maps are in the glove compartments of our cars, on our phones, in the newspaper, on hospital walls, and on the streets. It is hard to imagine a world without maps: indeed, without maps, it is hard to imagine a world.

What did we do before maps? Well, we had many other mechanisms to describe place and boundaries. The most important was language; people described where things were by referencing common ideas and objects. This conversation involved both telling and asking about place and detail. Your maps are in conversation with your users. With computer-based mapping, especially web mapping, interactivity allows the map to talk back to the user, whether it be a pop up with more detailed information, by being able to zoom out to see more of the world, or a hint on what is nearby. Your map should be a lucid, truthful, and friendly conversationalist.

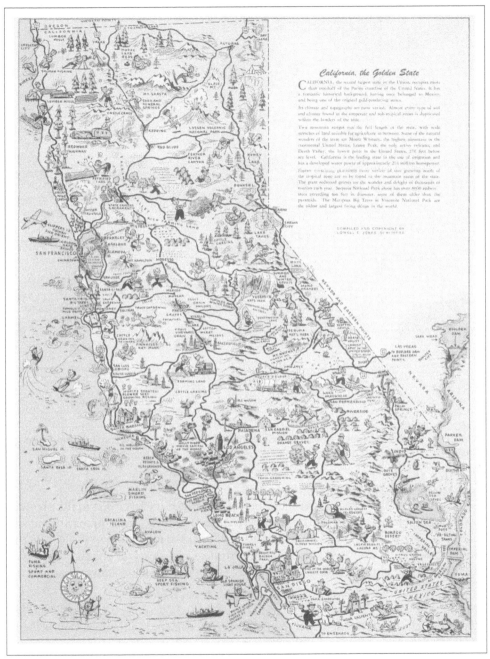

Figure 1-2. California, the Golden State, found at downtown.losbangeles.com (http://downtown .losbangeles.com/post/8108354451/california-the-golden-state-194)

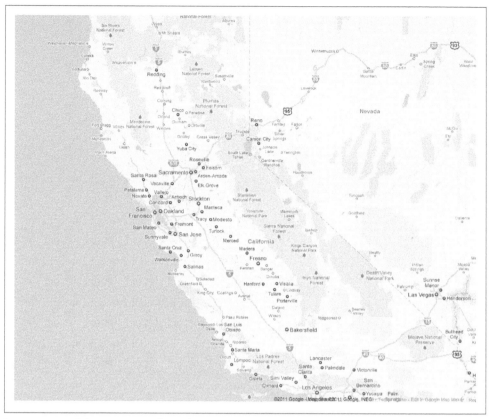

Figure 1-3. California as seen from the Road Map layer on maps.google.com (http://maps.google .com/)

Why Use Maps

So why map at all, and why make maps on your website? As described in the previous sections, mapping is not an inherently objective way to display data: maps are a mechanism for having a conversation, telling a story, or persuading; a map is a communication tool and an art. Still, it is important to decide if this will enhance your web application, and ultimately give your users a better experience, whatever that may be. Maps *can* be a bad idea.

Think about your audience. Does your audience know how to use a web map? Google Maps has defined the modern web mapping experience, and in doing so has brought many Internet users to this common map interface. Still, not all of your audience may be capable of navigating this interface. Keep this in mind if you are adding on new interactive features to a map: what makes it more useful to many will also make it more incomprehensible to some.

Does your data have geographical relevance? In general, if your data mentions place names, creating a map to explore that data will enhance the user experience. A map, coupled with a more traditional keyword search, can provide a more visual exploration method for your users. If your content is very geographically significant, for instance bus stops and times, a map may be almost necessary for users to understand the data.

Even if you have geographical data and an audience that can manage a web map interface, you will still have to be able to make decisions around your map to ensure that the map conveys the story you want to tell. If you are not able to complete the goal of the map, through lack of design, not providing enough context, or inability to provide real interaction, it may be best to avoid a map so that your users are not distracted by it, and instead focus on other methods for telling the story.

What Maps to Use

With web mapping, most people do not have the resources to create map tiles themselves, or even to host tiles (for detail on map tiles, see "Mapping Terms" on page 129). Later in the book we will discuss recent developments in open source mapping that have made these things more accessible. But even so, it is likely that you will need to use the map tiles of other map makers, such as Google, Bing, or MapQuest. They are not all the same. There are clear differences in the technical implementation, visual design, and the commercial and legal considerations. But beyond this there are different assumptions made by the maps and satellite imagery.

The following images show the difference in tile sets of road data in Stockholm (Figure 1-4) and the satellite imagery over the Horn of Africa (Figure 1-5). You can see that there are differences in data, design, and filtering.

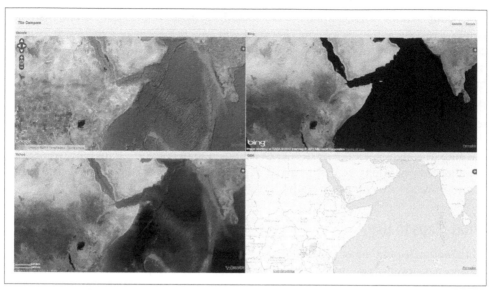

Figure 1-5. Satellite tiles over the Horn of Africa from Google, Bing, and Yahoo, as seen at Tile Compare (http://maps.zzolo.org/tile-compare/)

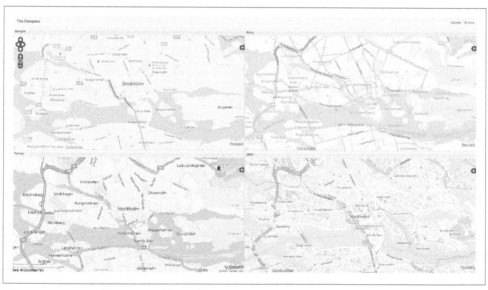

Figure 1-4. Street tiles over Stockholm from Google, Bing, Yahoo, and OpenStreetMap, as seen at Tile Compare (http://maps.zzolo.org/tile-compare/)

Further Resources

Critical cartography is a new term describing a new sort of thoughtful cartography (mapmaking) that carefully considers the effects of maps. When it comes to mapping, it is important to think: not just about where, but also about why and how. This will produce more exciting and useful maps for everyone. Not every Drupal map maker needs to be a deep thinker in the theory of cartography. But if you would like to get more into the philosophy of mapping, here are some useful and intriguing resources (more are in Appendix A):

- The Map Room Blog (*http://www.maproomblog.com/*)
- Radical Cartography (*http://radicalcartography.net/*)
- Strange Maps (*http://bigthink.com/blogs/strange-maps*)
- Rethinking the Power of Maps (*http://www.guilford.com/cgi-bin/cartscript.cgi?page =pr/wood.htm&dir=geo/tech&cart_id=36799.5999*)
- The Natures of Maps (*http://www.press.uchicago.edu/ucp/books/book/chicago/N/ bo5896623.html*)

The Power of Drupal

Given that we, indeed, do want mapping on our web application, why map with Drupal specifically? The number-one reason is that it is easy to get started with mapping in Drupal. As we will describe in this book, with just a couple modules and some clicking, you can have a simple map that tells your users the story of your data.

But the start is just the start. It gets complicated quite quickly. It's not the most straightforward thing to get Drupal maps that not only look good but are responsive, flexible, and robust. But then, that's not straightforward in any program or content management system. The great strength of Drupal is its relative simplicity, and its power to interact with content on your site and outside data sources.

Drupal as a CMS

That's the key: Drupal is a powerful Content Management System (CMS) that does a lot of heavy lifting for you. Drupal provides a robust, flexible way of managing content. And this is what we want to do with our maps; we want to tell stories about our content; we want to make art with our data. Going back to the earlier point about maps being a conversation: while your map is having a conversation with your user, your underlying data is also having a continuous real-time conversation with your mapping.

In Drupal 7 there is an abstract data concept called an *entity* that is a container for a specific sort of data, such as a user account, a blog post, or a restaurant. All entities can have fields, which are structured input mechanisms. Three possible fields for a restaurant entity could be names, addresses, and phone numbers. You can make almost any content in Drupal location-aware without any code, just by adding Drupal modules that provide geographic fields. With the right combination of modules, you can create maps that allow your users to find geographically relevant information.

We could go into more details as to why Drupal is a great option for web applications, but the assumption of this book is that you already want to use Drupal and are reading this to further your knowledge of how to map in Drupal.

 Mapping suites exist in other open source frameworks and languages. For a good alternative to Drupal for mapping and location data handling, check out GeoDjango (*http://geodjango.org/*), a geographical system for the Django framework. It is built on the Python programming language.

Mapping in Drupal

Drupal was one of the earliest content management systems to integrate with external mapping services. The first of these services to be integrated was the Google Maps API in 2005, through the Location and GMap modules. These modules have gained a lot of traction over the years and are still being developed in Drupal 7. In recent years, another approach to mapping in Drupal has centered around the OpenLayers and Geofield modules. The differences between these two approaches will be discussed in Chapter 3, and throughout the rest of the book the tutorials will cover both methods where possible.

Whichever of these methods you use for making maps, they both query spatial information from a database, then use JavaScript to display that information on a map. There are challenges in doing this with large amounts of data, since spatial database queries are slow and web browsers can only handle a limited amount of JavaScript. These challenges will be detailed in Chapter 2, and in the following chapters we will discuss ways of overcoming them.

Web Mapping Basics

Many people making web-based maps do not come from a geographical information system (GIS) or traditional mapmaking background, and can go years without knowing what a map projection is. This chapter will introduce map projections, data storage, and the challenges of making maps online.

If you just want to start working through the tutorials and making maps, feel free to skim over this chapter and come back to it later. That said, even trained geographers often have to pause to remember which is latitude and which is longitude. While it is not necessary to understand these concepts to make maps with Drupal, there will be a time when it is really helpful. Is all the GPS data that you imported showing up a few meters out of place? You're probably using mismatched projections. Is your map of Washington, DC, showing up in Antarctica? Your latitude and longitude are probably reversed. The first bug (*http://drupal.org/node/33951*) reported for the GMap module in Drupal in October 2005 was because the developer got this wrong.

 There are many mnemonics to help remember which is which. A common one is "lat is flat": on a normal map, the lines of latitude run east-west across the map and look horizontal or flat.

Projections and Coordinate Systems

The world is roughly spherical, but computer screens are flat. How we represent the world on a two-dimensional surface and how we locate ourselves and objects on it are difficult problems, and there are many different ways to handle these issues. A *map projection* is a way of representing the Earth on a flat surface, and a *coordinate system* is a way of describing a place on a map. These are difficult concepts to fully understand, but they affect how your maps look, how they get used, and how you create maps from a technical standpoint.

Map Projections

> A map projection is any method of representing the surface of a sphere or other three-dimensional body on a plane.
>
> —Wikipedia (*http://en.wikipedia.org/wiki/Map_projection*)

This representation is not a simple task and it has consequences depending on the method used. Ideally, we want to depict the territory of, for example, Europe on a flat piece of paper or screen so as to preserve shapes, directions, and bearings, and uniformly reduce area and distance. Sadly, there is no way to preserve all these properties. The variety of map projections are different ways of preserving some of these properties while sacrificing others.

For example, the Mercator projection has the property of preserving shapes and directions. However, it does this at the cost of enlarging all lands the further they are from the equator. Many people therefore get the impression that Greenland is about the same size as South America. Developing nations tend to be close to the equator, and their inhabitants often resent the Mercator projection, which makes Europe and North America appear much more significant in relative area than they are. Some of these objectors prefer the Equal-Area or Gall-Peters Projections, which are two different ways of representing the Earth that maintain the correct areas; the trade-off being distorting shapes—Iceland, for instance, looks like a stretched-out lens. Depending on what your map wants to communicate, it is important to choose a projection that will help your message. It is impossible to say what projection is best for your case, but it is important to consider what the projection communicates. No projection will be perfect, but one could be more appropriate for your audience than another.

In web mapping you are relying on the maps provided by Google, Bing, OpenStreetMap, or a similar service, and as a consequence there are only one or two projections available to use. The Spherical Mercator projection is the most common web mapping projection. This is probably what you will be using for your maps, but keep in mind the effect that the projection has on your map. If you need to map Antarctica, the Mercator projection assigns this continent an infinite area!

Some different map projections of the Earth are shown in Figure 2-1, Figure 2-2, Figure 2-3, and Figure 2-4. These are just a sample of projections to illustrate the impact that this choice has on a map.

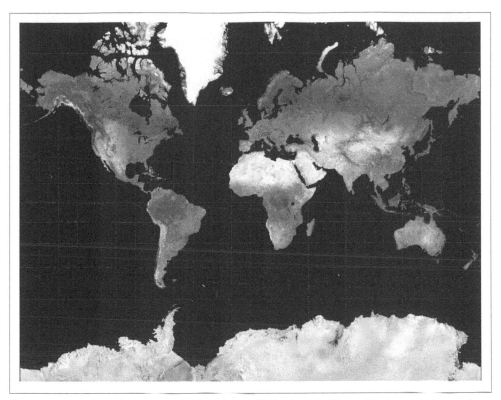

Figure 2-1. A Spherical Mercator projection of NASA's Blue Marble satellite imagery. Image from Learn NC (http://www.learnnc.org/lp/multimedia/14596)

Spherical Mercator

The Mercator projection is one of the most common projections. A variant of it, Spherical Mercator, is used by all major web-based maps (including Google, Bing, MapQuest, and OpenStreetMap). It makes the assumption that the Earth is a perfect sphere (though it is not). As shown in the illustration (Figure 2-5), the method of flattening the globe is to spread out the globe onto a cylinder. Imagine a translucent world with a very bright lightbulb at the exact center and its image projected onto the cylinder. This means that areas close to the equator are fairly accurate, but as you get further toward the poles, the areas are very enlarged. This illustrates the problem with all map projections: it is impossible to have all four aspects of a map be accurate (direction, distance, area, shape). In fact, you can't get more than two. Mercator is good for direction and shape.

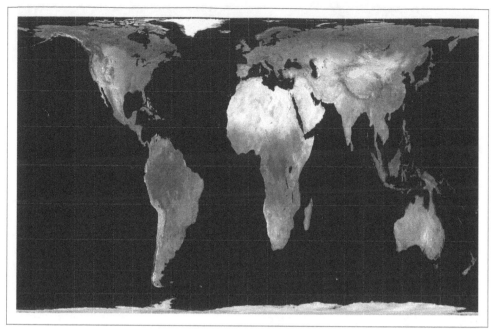

Figure 2-2. A Gall-Peters projection of NASA's Blue Marble satellite imagery (image from Wikipedia (http://en.wikipedia.org/wiki/File:Gall-peters.jpg))

  If you are working with geographic data sets, you may come across numbers that refer to their data projection. Projections have been given identification numbers by the European Petroleum Survey Group (EPSG; now the International Association of Oil & Gas Producers). These identification numbers are often used by different tools to designate projections. The Spherical Mercator projection, temporarily given EPSG:900913, is now officially EPSG:3857. (If you are familiar with leet speak (*http://en.wikipedia.org/wiki/Leet*), you would notice that 900913 looks like the word Google (*http://crschmidt.net/blog/archives/243/goo gle-projection-900913/*)). Another common projection is the projection that translates to latitude and longitude, which is EPSG:4326.

More resources

Although Spherical Mercator is the projection that is most common in web mapping, there are a theoretically limitless number of other map projections. It is important to understand a bit about projections from a technical standpoint and the effects they can have on your maps and your map users. Other map projections are covered in more depth in Appendix B. In addition to this, there is some useful information online:

- Wikipedia has a thorough article on map projections (*http://en.wikipedia.org/wiki/ Map_projection*).

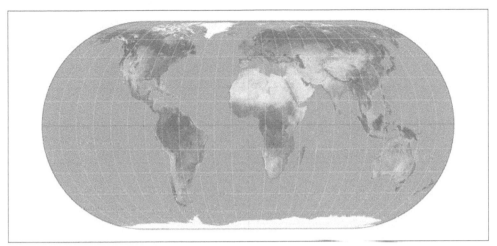

Figure 2-3. An Ecker IV projection (image from Wikipedia (http://en.wikipedia.org/wiki/File:Ecker _IV_projection_SW.jpg))

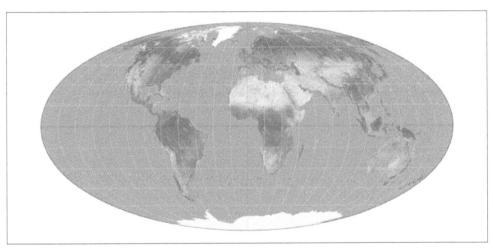

Figure 2-4. A Mollweide projection (image from Wikipedia (http://en.wikipedia.org/wiki/File: Mollweide_projection_SW.jpg))

- Mapthematics has a really interesting visualization of the effects of projection (*http: //www.mapthematics.com/Projections/Images/Cornucopia33.jpg*).

- Mapthematics also has an in-depth look at projections (*http://www.mapthematics .com/Essentials.php*).

- Mapthematics provides a list of projections (*http://www.mapthematics.com/Projec tionsList.php*) and details about each.

- Kartoweb has an even more in-depth look at projections (*http://kartoweb.itc.nl/ geometrics/Map%20projections/Understanding%20Map%20Projections.pdf*).

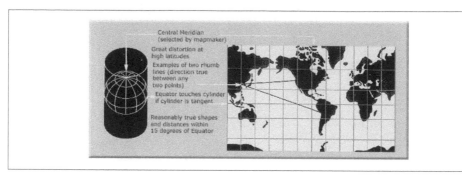

Figure 2-5. Mercator Projection, courtesy of the U.S. Geological Survey

- Wikipedia has a good overview of the World Geodetic System projection (*http://en.wikipedia.org/wiki/World_Geodetic_System*).

Further reading is listed in Appendix A.

Coordinate Systems

A coordinate system is a way of referring to a location with a set of numbers. The coordinates that are most important for web-based maps are latitude and longitude. Latitude is the angular distance north or south from the equator. Latitudes north of the equator are positive; latitudes south of the equator are negative. Longitude is the east-west position of a point, and is also expressed as an angle. The latitude of zero runs north-south through the Royal Observatory at Greenwich in the UK. Places east of this have positive values and west are negative.

When setting up maps in Drupal, developers run into a surprising number of problems caused by mixing up latitude and longitude or mixing positive and negative values for latitude. If you ever come across your map of public toilets in Paris unexpectedly showing you some ocean west of the continent of Africa (Figure 2-6), this is the point where both latitude and longitude are zero, which usually means that your map is not receiving the location data or there is some projection issue.

Figure 2-6. The location of 0,0 shown on OpenStreetMap

Latitude and longitude are normally measured in degrees, minutes, and seconds. A sphere has 360 degrees. Each degree can be divided into 60 minutes (referring to the angle, not time). Each minute can be divided into 60 seconds. For example, New York City is at 40° 43′ 0″ North, 74° 0′ 0″ West. This is often turned into a pair of decimal numbers for web mapping or mathematical calculations: 40.716667, -74.

Longitude first

Most of us usually recite coordinates as latitude first, then longitude second. This order is arbitrary and makes things harder for web-based mapping, so often you will see APIs using longitude first.

Web mapping, specifically, tile-based mapping (see "Mapping Terms" on page 129 for more details on tile-based mapping) presents a unique problem: how does one take into account, map tile positions, viewport positions, and actual map coordinates? Computer applications, specifically with HTML and CSS, make the assumption that the position that is most top and left is a (0,0) point, and that positive numbers represent going down and right respectively. This means that tile sets are usually formed like Z/X/Y.png. The Z is the zoom level, and the X and the Y represent where the tile image fits into the map starting from top left. This then leads to web mapping libraries basing a lot of calculations on this top/left or x,y system. Also, when you start to look at latitude and longitude, the longitude value would be on the x-axis and latitude would be on the y-axis, and computers usually use a Cartesian x,y coordinate system. So, that is why we often see longitude first in web mapping.

Data Storage

There are a number of open source and proprietary storage systems for geospatial data, and there are just as many standards for how to represent the data. We will go through some of the basics here, but this is a large topic that we cannot cover completely. The Open Geospatial Consortium (*http://www.opengeospatial.org/*) (OGC) is a well-established body that helps define many of the open standards used in geographic information systems. It is helpful to understand these concepts as you decide on the best way to gather and store information to display on your map.

Data Types

There are two main data types when talking about geospatial data: *vector* (such as points and lines) and *raster* (such as satellite imagery).

Vector data

Most often, geospatial data is represented as geometric shapes and stored sets of numbers representing these shapes; these are most commonly *points*, *lines*, or *polygons*.

Vector data standards

Three of the main geographic data storage types are shown in the table below (Table 2-1) for point data and polygon data (a shape), along with a text version. When we think about a place, typically we refer to its name, for example, *New York*. But this is not very useful when we try to do calculations or comparisons. What do we mean when we say New York? Are we talking about the city? The state? The borough of Manhattan? And nothing in the names *Shanghai* and *Sydney* is any help in determining where they are or what the distance is between them. Representing a location with numbers (for example latitude and longitude) removes this ambiguity.

A location as a latitude and longitude is not always useful, though. It is just a single point. Sometimes we need to represent a shape, normally referred to as a polygon in mapping. Only polygon data can answer questions like "Is Manhattan an island?" Whereas point data can be described as two separate fields in a database, polygons require more complicated data storage types, such as *Well Known Text* (WKT) and *Keyhole Markup Language* (KML).

WKT is a versatile format, because it is text that can be read and stored very easily. It is supported in Drupal by the Geofield module (*http://drupal.org/project/geofield*), and is used in the tutorials in "Geofield Module" on page 29. As is shown in Table 2-1, WKT is flexible in the type of geographic data it can handle: it can be used to represent a single point with just one latitude and longitude; it can represent a line (a series of points); or it can represent a polygon (a line that connects at each end).

KML is a file format used to display geographic data using a structure that is based on XML. It is widely used because of its support in Google Maps and Google Earth. As a file format it is not suited to being stored in a database. Instead, it is useful when you want to share geographic information with other websites and applications, especially if you do not need to update this information frequently. Using KML files on your maps is covered in "Creating an OpenLayers Map Layer from KML" on page 59, and creating KML files is described in the tutorial in "Creating Feeds" on page 67.

There are many other geographic data formats. *GPX* and *TCX* are based on XML. They are formats used by *GPS* (global positioning systems) devices to track routes and way points. *GeoJSON* is based on *JSON* (JavaScript Object Notation), which is generally more compact than XML. Like WKT, GeoJSON is able to represent many different geographic data types.

Table 2-1. Data standards examples

Standards	Point Data (New York City)	Polygon Data (border of Manhattan)
Descriptive Text	New York City, New York	Borough of Manhattan, New York
Longitude/ Latitude	-74, 40.71	n/a

Well Known Text (WKT)	`POINT(-74, 40.71)`	`POLYGON((`
		`    -73.924942016601 40.877698964746,`
		`    -73.909149169922 40.8709493023,`
		`    -73.934555053711 40.828878212816,`
		`    -73.927688598633 40.798736824942,`
		`    -73.975067138672 40.712394426605,`
		`    -74.020385742188 40.698340181788,`
		`    -74.010086059571 40.75193859846,`
		`    -73.924942016601 40.877698964746`
		`))`

Keyhole Markup Language (KML)	``` <kml xmlns= "http://www.opengis.net/kml/2.2" xmlns:kml= "http://www.opengis.net/kml/2.2" xmlns:gx= "http://www.google.com/kml/ext/2.2" xmlns:atom= "http://www.w3.org/2005/Atom"> <Placemark> <name>New York, NY</name> <address>New York, NY</address> <Point> <coordinates> -74.005973,40.714353,0 </coordinates> </Point> </Placemark> </kml> ```	``` <kml xmlns= "http://www.opengis.net/kml/2.2" xmlns:kml= "http://www.opengis.net/kml/2.2" xmlns:gx= "http://www.google.com/kml/ext/2.2" xmlns:atom= "http://www.w3.org/2005/Atom"> <Placemark> <name>Manhattan</name> <Polygon> <outerBoundaryIs> <LinearRing> <coordinates> -74.01329346663975, 40.74552522927475,0 -74.01417775693378, 40.70205660546712,0 -73.97852222542525, 40.70941144929174,0 -73.97336836375017, 40.72746020668423,0 -73.97442958078742, 40.74197149381666,0 -73.93018494756411, 40.79937286781991,0 -73.93626079695892, 40.83462951863233,0 -73.92487861077853, 40.85468660366949,0 -73.93505410575875, 40.85845257892458,0 -74.01329346663975, 40.74552522927475,0 </coordinates> </LinearRing> </outerBoundaryIs> </Polygon> </Placemark> </kml> ```

Raster data

The other main way of representing and storing geospatial data is in raster format. This is the idea of storing data as a continuous surface, a grid of pixels. Raster data is most often a digital image, or set of digital images; it can be satellite imagery, or it could be an image of a street map, but the pixels can represent any value. Elevation is a good example of the difference between vector and raster data; using vector format, elevation is represented with contour lines, but in raster format, it is a *digital elevation model* (DEM), a continuous surface with each pixel equal to the elevation averaged across the pixel (see Figure 2-7). Digital imagery provides a very efficient way of displaying a lot of data in a fast format. It is also very stable; it looks the same in any browser.

Figure 2-7. A Digital Elevation Model map of the Sierra Nevada mountain range (image from Wikipedia (http://en.wikipedia.org/wiki/File:Maps-for-free_Sierra_Nevada.png))

Almost all modern web mapping uses a system of tiles (images) to provide a "Slippy Map" (pioneered by Google Maps). A "Slippy Map" is an interface where a map is displayed inside a rectangle of a particular fixed size, a *viewport*. You can drag the map around while remaining in that viewport and the page does not need to reload to display new sections of the map. The mechanics of this interface are based on map information stored as a set of sliced-up images (*map tiles*). These tiles can be loaded on demand depending on which part of the map the user is viewing, and at what zoom level. A tile set can be huge; a world map supporting a typical 256×256 image size with 18 zoom levels (at which point a baseball or football stadium fills a typical laptop screen) leads to billions of tiles. Map tiles for Drupal are discussed and illustrated later in "Map Tiles" on page 109.

Raster tile sets are also often generated from vector data. Tile sets from map providers like Google or Bing use their database of roads and points of interest to create raster tile sets for users to put into their application. Another example is OpenStreetMap (*http://www.openstreetmap.org/*), which provides a wiki for users all over the world to add geospatial data describing the world around them to a single vector database. OpenStreetMap is actually just the vector data—the roads and paths and points of interests, all of which is released under a license for anyone to reuse. Anyone can use this data to create raster images. The OpenStreetMap organization also produces some tile sets for people to use in their applications.

Databases

Mapping applications that need to perform spatial calculations (for example to produce a map that shows all whiskey bars within one mile of my office) will use a database that stores data in a spatial format. A spatial database is optimized to store and query geographic information, so it will be faster, for instance, to measure a distance between two points, to return all points within an area or radius, or check if two areas intersect. PostGIS (*http://postgis.org/*) does this for PostgreSQL databases, and MySQL has spatial extensions (*http://dev.mysql.com/doc/refman/5.0/en/spatial-extensions.html*) available.

Currently no Drupal 7 modules support spatial databases. Instead they store geographic data in the database as text or integers (numbers). This is a good solution for a typical Drupal installation, as most mapping websites do not need the most demanding operations. This does make it difficult and cumbersome to do spatial calculations, such as finding what lines intersect, or what points or in a polygon, or what whiskey bars are close to you.

Drupal 7's database abstraction layer makes it easier to support databases other than MySQL, but there has been only a little work done to develop geographic modules that take advantage of this. The PostGIS module (*http://drupal.org/sandbox/geops/1212962*) integrates with the OpenLayers module (*http://drupal.org/project/openlayers*) and allows geographic features to be stored natively in a spatial database, but it does not attempt to provide a way to do spatial queries. The Geo module (*http://drupal.org/project/geo*) provides both support for spatial databases and queries in Drupal 6, but it has not yet been upgraded to Drupal 7.

Despite the limitations of not having deep integration with spatial databases, Drupal can handle most mapping storage and calculations. The main limitation is doing calculations with complex shapes. Calculating what places are within a rectangle or circle is possible, but determining what falls within an arbitrary shape is more difficult. Similarly, calculating whether a shape that a user draws on a map overlaps with another shape (such as a voting district) is beyond the current capabilities of mapping in Drupal 7.

Given the lack of support for spatial databases in Drupal 7, most mapping applications in Drupal just use a standard MySQL database. This is suitable in most cases, but creates some challenges.

Challenges of Web-Based Mapping

The difficulties of making a map to be used online can be grouped into a couple of areas: there are limits to how much data a web browser can display on a typical interactive map, and there are usability problems when trying to display large amounts of information on a map.

Browser Capabilities

Most interactive maps use JavaScript very heavily. The image tiles that make up the map are loaded using JavaScript as the user zooms in and out and moves around the map. The points, lines, and polygons displayed on the map are added with JavaScript (usually interacting with HTML Canvas or SVG). Even modern web browsers have a point at which they get overwhelmed and become unresponsive because the client cannot handle all of the processing. A good rule of thumb for the limitation of points (including vertices in a polygon) is around 200–500. But, as this is client-side processing, performance varies depending on the user's browser and hardware, so you should take into account your audience when determining these limitations.

 There is no hard limitation, as the limitation comes from the client (the browser and hardware of the user's computer, phone, tablet, etc.). Modern browsers, such as Chrome, can handle upwards of 10,000 points, while Internet Explorer 7 is more like 300. Unfortunately, there have been no benchmarks for this, as there are so many variables to consider.

Client-side clustering

One approach to lessen the load on the client is to use a form of *clustering*. If there are a large number of points in close proximity, they will be grouped together, and this grouping will normally be represented by a different style of marker. What happens when this "group" marker is clicked depends on the clustering tool. Either the map may zoom in to show all the separate points in that area, or the group marker may load a pop up displaying a list of all the points that it contains. This helps the browser not have to render all the markers or features, and it will save some resources. However the clustering is done by JavaScript in the browser, so this will not lead to a huge increase in performance.

Library size

A second approach is to use less demanding JavaScript. By lessening the amount of JavaScript that the client has to download, and minimizing the amount of processing on the client in order for you to achieve the map you want, you can squeeze some more performance out of your maps.

One example is Modest Maps (*https://github.com/stamen/modestmaps-js*). This is a very lightweight JavaScript API for displaying map tiles. By focusing on displaying map tiles and not providing any default markers or buttons for navigating the map, the Modest Maps JavaScript file is 28 KB, compared to over 700 KB for the OpenLayers JavaScript and around 150 KB for the Google Maps JavaScript API. However, the trade off is that you do not have a very full-featured API available.

One company that decided to make this trade off is Development Seed (*http://develop mentseed.org/*). Development Seed has worked with open source web-based mapping for years and contributed a lot to many Drupal modules. They switched from primarily using the OpenLayers JavaScript library to using Modest Maps (*http://modestmaps .com/*). They wrote their own library for the interaction and map widgets to go on top of this, called Wax (*https://github.com/mapbox/wax*), and in doing so they reduced file size by 70%. Although there is this considerable improvement in file size, the significant trade off is that Modest Maps and most of the other newer mapping APIs do not yet have integration with Drupal.

 Recently, CloudMade (*http://cloudmade.com/*) released an open source JavaScript mapping library called Leaflet (*http://leaflet.cloudmade .com/*). It is simple and lightweight. There is also a new Leaflet module (*http://drupal.org/project/leaflet*) for Drupal that provides some basic integration between Drupal and Leaflet. It is something to keep an eye on.

Tile rendering

The other way to work around web browser limitations in creating maps is to render your data as raster imagery (see "Raster data" on page 20).

Until recently this required a thorough understanding of complex and/or expensive GIS software. This barrier has been reduced by two recent new technologies. The first of these is TileMill (*http://tilemill.com*), which is open source software for designing maps and creating map tiles that integrate with various mapping APIs.

TileMill allows you to load in a large dataset containing spatial data and turn it into map tiles. The data could be points, such as locations of health centers, or shapes, such as outlines of states in the US. They can be rendered on the tiles in different colors to represent the data. And despite rendering the data into the map tiles, people can still click on the map to get more information about the data. TileMill and other ways of creating tiles are discussed in "Map Tiles" on page 109.

While using TileMill allows web maps to display massive data sets, the trade off is that the tiles that are generated need to be hosted (an extra expense) and the maps can only contain the information that is available when the tiles were created. It is difficult to display current information in the same way that would be possible if the information was being pulled straight from a database. Every time you update the data you must rerender all the tiles. If you are mapping incidents of violence during civil unrest, you do not want to wait a day or a week to update your map.

The other interesting new technology that uses tile rendering to display large data sets is Google's Fusion Tables (*http://code.google.com/apis/maps/articles/toomanymarkers .html#fusiontables*). Using the Google Maps JavaScript API, you can query data and map tiles are rendered on the fly to display that data. Currently, though, there is no integration in Drupal for Fusion Tables.

Usability

Large amounts of data are a problem for the web browser, and are also a problem for people looking at the map. A map with hundreds of markers covering it is overwhelming. Too much information is as bad as too little. Indeed, it is worse, as it takes longer to load!

Another problem happens when the map is trying to display several pieces of information at the same location, for example, showing three businesses in the same building on different floors. With a standard configuration it is impossible to access more than one marker. Clustering, discussed earlier, is one way to deal with this. The other way is to manage what data is displayed and to give users different ways to refine this, for example by using exposed filters in views, or detecting a user's location and showing them what is nearby. This is discussed in Chapter 4.

As more people access websites through mobile browsers on tablets and smartphones, it is important to consider the user experience for this audience. In other words, keep the maps you build simple, so that the information can be seen on small screens and so that the maps load quickly. The latest versions of the APIs for both Google Maps (V3 Maps API) and OpenLayers (2.11) have added a lot of improvements for using maps on mobile devices. They have made the maps faster, have added support for touch screens (such as zooming in and out by pinching the screen), and integrated geolocation to show where a user is on the map.

In some cases a map is not the best interface for geographic data, whether because of the size of the data set or because people can not access visual information due to a visual impairment. For both accessibility and search engine optimization, it is often worth creating alternative text-based ways of displaying the same data. The Views module (*http://drupal.org/project/views*) in Drupal makes this straightforward. A map is just one display type in Views; you can provide the same information as a list or table. This is covered in "Other Ways of Displaying Spatial Data" on page 65.

CHAPTER 3

Spatial Data

Before you can display a map, you need to get spatial data into your site in some way. Drupal gives you many options for modules and data formats to use. This chapter provides an overview of these and outlines the strengths and weaknesses of each. Four aspects of dealing with spatial data will be covered: how the data is stored in Drupal, how the data is input by users, how the data is manipulated, and how it can be queried.

> Many modules handle several aspects of data storage, manipulation, and display, so you will notice the same modules in several sections of this chapter and the rest of the book.

Drupal has a vibrant community of contributors, and this translates to many different modules and approaches to similar problems. This is great for promoting innovation and solving specific needs, but can make it difficult for site builders to work out the best solutions for their particular problems. This chapter will not be able to cover all the possibilities for spatial data in Drupal, but it will give you an in-depth look at the more established methods.

> The Drupal Mapping Group (*http://groups.drupal.org/location-and -mapping*) has a wiki page that describes the different geospatial modules (*http://groups.drupal.org/node/89769*) and is the best place to get an overview of the modules available for your geospatial needs.

Data Storage

Different data formats for spatial data were introduced in "Data Storage" on page 17. This section will introduce the different *modules* and approaches for working with those data formats, and work through tutorials for implementing these with Drupal.

If you are unfamiliar with Drupal terminology like *module* and *node,* you can look them up online in the Drupal glossary (*http://drupal.org/ glossary*).

Database Layer in Drupal

Drupal 7 offers a powerful and adaptable database abstraction layer. The abstraction layer allows developers to write database queries and modules that will work on different types of databases. Drupal aims to support MySQL, Postgres, and SQLite. Other database, such as Microsoft SQL Server and Oracle, can be supported by installing contributed modules.

Drupal core has a huge amount of inline documentation in the code, which is automatically parsed and collected on Drupal's API reference website (*http://api.drupal.org*). This includes a page on the database abstraction layer (*http://api.drupal.org/api/group/database/7*). There is also lots of community-sourced documentation on the database documentation page (*http://drupal.org/developing/api/database*).

As discussed in "Data Storage" on page 17, spatial databases have specific data types to handle geographical features, and they provide specific querying ability for spatial data. Unfortunately Drupal does not natively support these data types or these querying methods, so there are a number of contributed modules to solve this problem.

There is currently a ticket in the Drupal issue queue to add support for spatial data. Feel free to help out or just show your support by commenting on the ticket (*http://drupal.org/node/293483*).

Methods

There are two main methods for storing spatial data in Drupal 7: one is with the Geofield module (*http://drupal.org/project/geofield*), and the other is the Location module (*http: //drupal.org/project/location*). The rest of this chapter and Chapter 4 will illustrate the differences between the Geofield and Location modules and help you choose the correct approach for your maps.

Please be aware that the methods outlined in this chapter are not interchangeable. They all store the spatial data in their own ways. This means that you should think carefully right at the start about what kind of spatial data you want to store and what you will need to do with it. Halfway through is too late to decide that you want to input the routes of your mountain bike rides and should have been using Geofield rather than Location!

Geofield

The Geofield module (*http://drupal.org/project/geofield*) is a new module that was created for Drupal 7. Geofield allows geographical data to be attached to an *entity*, such as a *node*. It provides several different *widgets* for data input and *formatters* for data output. It integrates with several of the other popular mapping modules (including OpenLayers, GMap, and Geocoder), and there are plans to integrate with more.

Of all the modules that handle geographic data storage in Drupal 7, the Geofield module is the one that has seen most development recently and takes the most advantage of the new *Fields API*. For these reasons, it is the best choice for all but the simplest mapping applications.

For data storage the Geofield module can be configured to handle many formats:

Latitude and Longitude
> Data can be entered either as *Decimal Degrees* (122.340932) or as *Degrees-Minutes-Seconds* (123° 49' 55.2" W). The Degrees-Minutes-Seconds input is tolerant of inconsistent input (123° 49' 55.2" W or 40:26:46N). Decimal Degrees is what you are most likely to be using.

Bounding Box
> The latitude and longitude of each corner of a rectangle can be entered in four text fields.

Well Known Text (WKT)
> A text area for direct WKT input (see "Data Types" on page 17 for an explanation of WKT).

In addition to these formats, the Geofield module can store data for points, lines, polygons, and bounding boxes drawn on a map by a user. Geofield can integrate with the Geocoder module (*http://drupal.org/project/geocoder*) to store spatial data that has been extracted from addresses, KML files, GeoJSON data, and geotagged images. This is discussed in "Geocoder and Addressfield" on page 41.

Location

The Location module (*http://drupal.org/project/location*) has been around since Drupal 4.6 in 2005 and is one of the oldest spatial modules for Drupal. The Location module allows spatial data (such as a full address or latitude and longitude) to be attached to nodes and users.

The Location module's strengths include an established interface; the interface of this module may not be perfect, but it has been around long enough for most Drupal users to have come across it at some point. Location is also quite full-featured, handling address data from around the world, as well as plugging into geocoding services.

Of course, "full-featured" also means that the module can be heavy and may load lots of functionality you do not need. A more serious drawback is that the Location module does not allow for line or polygon spatial data types. You can only store simple point data (a single latitude and longitude for each location). You will not be able to make a map that shows hiking routes or the area affected by an oil spill.

The architecture (how the code is written) of the Location module, which was appropriate when it was first conceived, does not follow current Drupal conventions. For example, it stores locations in a separate table and attaches them to entities like nodes and users with custom code, as opposed to using the Fields API, which is the best practice in Drupal 7. The Location module cannot currently attach spatial information to any entities other than users and nodes.

 The developers of the Location module are planning a new version of the module that will handle location data as entities. You can follow the progress of this in the Location module's issue queue (*http://drupal.org/ node/1346746*).

Despite these drawbacks, there are two good reasons to use the Location module. If you are upgrading a site from Drupal 6 or earlier that uses the Location module, it will be easier to keep your data in the same format. Additionally, as will be discussed in Chapter 4, it is quicker and simpler to create maps based on the Location module than it is to use Geofield.

Text fields

Text fields are a very simple, yet valid, way of storing spatial data in Drupal. All that is needed are two text fields to store latitude and longitude. As will be discussed in Chapter 4, most mapping modules are able to use any fields that contain a latitude and longitude; these values do not need to come from the Geofield or Location module.

The downside is that it is not very flexible or extensible: there is no ability to do spatial querying on the data (e.g., to show all the schools within 20 miles of the nuclear power plant), and there is no way to store lines or polygons. Also, most users may only know the address of a location; they will not have a latitude and longitude. However, if you are importing spatial data from another source and already have a latitude and longitude, this can sometimes be the best method. Usually Geofield is better because it will allow you to do spatial calculations, as well as displaying your data on a map.

Geo

Though the Geo module (*http://drupal.org/project/geo*) does not exist for Drupal 7, it is still an important module conceptually. The main goal of Geo is to provide a robust interface between a spatial database such as PostGIS or MySQL and Drupal so as to fully use the capabilities of these storage engines in your Drupal application. Other modules are in progress to do this in Drupal 7. If you are going to create spatially complex and demanding maps, this subject is discussed in "The Future of Mapping with Drupal" on page 122.

Data Input

The Geofield and Location modules store spatial information in different ways, so the data must be input in different ways. The tutorials in this section show how to work with Drupal and these modules to collect and store spatial data.

Geofield Module

As explained in "Geofield" on page 27, the Geofield module has many different ways to collect spatial data. This tutorial will explain the simplest configuration, and will provide the basis for exploring more advanced techniques.

Basic configuration of Geofield

Setting up the Geofield module includes a few extra steps not normally followed when setting up a Drupal module. Geofield requires that you add the geoPHP (*http://geophp .net*) library. GeoPHP is an open source PHP library for doing spatial operations, such as converting geographic data from JSON to WKT or calculating the area of a polygon.

1. Download the latest stable release of the Geofield module (*http://drupal.org/ project/geofield*) to your site's modules directory.

2. Download the latest stable release of the Libraries module (*http://drupal.org/ project/libraries*) to your site's modules directory. The Libraries module is used by Drupal modules like Geofield that require a third-party library or plug-in.

3. If it is not already there, create a *libraries* directory inside your Drupal installation's *sites/all* directory.

4. Download the geoPHP library (*https://github.com/downloads/phayes/geoPHP/ge oPHP.tar.gz*) (alternatively, the *git* repository can be cloned, or it can be downloaded as a *zip* file from the project's github page (*https://github.com/phayes/geophp*)).

The geoPHP library, an open source library for doing geospatial operations, also aims to provide a transparent layer on top of the GEOS extension in PHP. *Geometry Engine, Open Source (http://trac .osgeo.org/geos/)* (GEOS) is a C++ port of the Java Topology Suite (JTS), which is an API for modelling and manipulating two-dimensional linear geometry; GEOS is extremely efficient in doing geospatial operations. This means that if you install GEOS on your server, you will get a significant performance increase and will be able to do some more serious geospatial operations within PHP that normally would be done in a geospatial database like PostGIS. For more information, see the GEOS wiki page at geoPHP (*https: //github.com/phayes/geoPHP/wiki/GEOS*).

5. Extract the downloaded geoPHP library and place it inside *sites/all/libraries*. The file should now show in your directory structure as *sites/all/libraries/geoPHP/geoPHP.inc*.

6. Enable the Geofield and Libraries modules at *admin/modules*. Neither of these modules require any further configuration or permissions.

Adding geographic data to a node with Geofield

The example website that we are building throughout this book contains information about the Drupal community. Right now we will create a new *content type* to store local user groups. The content type will contain the name of the group, a short description, and some geographical data about where the group is located.

1. From the Content types page, add a new content type at *admin/structure/types/add*.

2. Enter **User Group** as the Name.

3. Enter **A local Drupal user group** as the Description.

4. Change the "Title field label" to **Group name**.

5. All other options can remain as default for now. Click the "Save and add fields" button.

6. You are now taken to the "Manage fields" page for this content type at *admin/ structure/types/manage/user-group/fields*. The third field listed should be "Body." Click the "edit" link to change this.

7. Change the "Label" field from **Body** to **Group description**. All other fields can stay with the default values. Click the "Save settings" button.

8. On the "Manage fields" page, go to the "Add new field" row. Enter **Group location** as the Label and **group_location** as the Field name. In the "Select a field type" drop-down, choose "Geofield." In the Widget drop-down choose "OpenLayers map." Your configuration should now look like Figure 3-1.

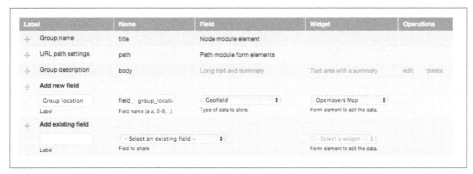

Label		Name	Field	Widget	Operations
⊹	Group name	title	Node module element		
⊹	URL path settings	path	Path module form elements		
⊹	Group description	body	Long text and summary	Text area with a summary	edit delete
⊹	**Add new field**				
	Group location	field_ group_locati	Geofield ⧫	Openlayers Map ⧫	
	Label	Field name (a-z, 0-9, _)	Type of data to store.	Form element to edit the data.	
⊹	**Add existing field**				
			– Select an existing field – ⧫	– Select a widget – ⧫	
	Label		Field to share	Form element to edit the data.	

Figure 3-1. Configuring the user group content type

9. Click the Save button at the bottom of the page to create this field.

10. You are first taken to the field level settings; there is no further configuration for this widget, so click "Save field settings" on the next screen.

11. On the final screen, tick the "Required field" checkbox so that a location has to be set for this content type. Enter some useful Help text, too: **Click on the map to set the location for this group**. There is currently just one option in the "OpenLayers Map" drop-down (Geofield Widget Map). As we go through the exercises in later chapters, more maps will be added to this list.

    It is possible to set a default location for nodes of this content type by clicking on the map in the "Default value" section, but this is not useful for this example. It is also possible to change the "Number of values" for the location field, but leave this set to 1 for this example. Click the "Save settings" button.

12. Create a sample "User Group." From the "Add Content" page at *node/add*, add a "User Group." Enter the name of the group (e.g., *New York City*). Enter a description for the group. Zoom in on the map and click to set the location of the group. This should look something like Figure 3-2.

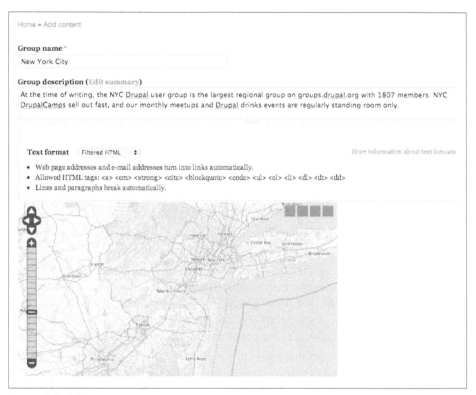

Home » Add content

Group name *

New York City

Group description (Edit summary)

At the time of writing, the NYC Drupal user group is the largest regional group on groups.drupal.org with 1807 members. NYC DrupalCamps sell out fast, and our monthly meetups and Drupal drinks events are regularly standing room only.

Text format   Filtered HTML ♦   More information about text formats

- Web page addresses and e-mail addresses turn into links automatically.
- Allowed HTML tags: \<a> \<em> \<strong> \<cite> \<blockquote> \<code> \<ul> \<ol> \<li> \<dl> \<dt> \<dd>
- Lines and paragraphs break automatically.

Figure 3-2. Adding content

13. Save the node.
14. When viewing this node, you'll see the location displaying something like "POINT (-73.9987036058 40.7345513658)." This is the location in Well Known Text (WKT) format, as described in "Data Types" on page 17. Unless you are a robot, this display isn't useful when searching for your local Drupal user group. To see what other display options are available, go to the "Manage Display" page for the User Group content type at *admin/structure/types/manage/user_group/display*.
15. In the "Format" column for the "Group location" field change the display from "Well Known Text (WKT)" to "OpenLayers."
16. Click on the cog symbol on the right side to open the configuration options for the field display. Again, at this point, the only available map is the one that comes with the Geofield module for this purpose, so select "Geofield Formatter Map." For the data option select "Use full geometry." It should look as shown in Figure 3-3. Click "Update" to save your settings, then click "Save."

New York City

View Edit

Submitted by tom_o_t on Mon, 10/03/2011 - 14:37

At the time of writing, the NYC Drupal user group is the largest regional group on groups.drupal.org with 1807 members. NYC DrupalCamps sell out fast, and our monthly meetups and Drupal drinks events are regularly standing room only.

Group location:

Figure 3-4. A location displayed on a map

Figure 3-3. Configuring Geofield display settings

17. Go to the content management page at *admin/content/node* and view the "User Group" content that you have just created. The location should now be shown as a dot at the center of a map, as shown in Figure 3-4.

Congratulations! You now have a content type configured to collect spatial data using a point-and-click map interface. The information that is collected for a node is then displayed on a map.

Location Module

As mentioned in "Location" on page 27, when using the Location module, spatial information can only be attached to nodes and users. In this example we will create a new content type that will be used as a business listing for Drupal development companies.

Basic configuration of location

The Location module is fairly simple to configure, but it is important to understand which of the included modules to use. At the time of publication, there is not a stable release of the Location module for Drupal 7, but the development version works fine.

1. Download the latest development release of the Location module (*http://drupal .org/project/location*) to your site's modules directory.

> The Location module that you download contains several modules, two of which will be used in this example.
>
> Confusingly, the Location module contains both the Node Location module and the Location CCK module. You should probably just ignore the Node Location module.
>
> These two modules both allow a location to be attached to a node in different ways: the Node Location module is a relic of the way that modules worked in Drupal 4.7 and Drupal 5 and does not use the Fields API (or CCK in Drupal 6). If you use the Node Location module, the location form will show up in the vertical tabs at the bottom of the node adding form.
>
> The Location CCK module takes advantage of the Fields API (or CCK in Drupal 6) and is usually the better option to use unless you are upgrading an old site and want a simpler migration process. It is usually a bad idea to enable both modules, as it can be confusing, and if you accidentally enable both methods of collecting location on a particular content type, the location data will be not be stored. More information about this is in the Location module issue queue (*http://drupal.org/node/906968*), and also in the *IN-STALL.txt* file in the Location module.

2. Enable two modules at *admin/modules*: the Location and Location CCK modules.
3. Configure permissions for the Location module at *admin/people/permissions#module-location*. The first three permissions should only be assigned to the *Administrator* role, but the "Submit latitude/longitude" permission will need to be given to the *Authenticated User* role. Click the "Save permissions" button.

If you ever need people to enter a location before they have an account on your site, remember to give the "Submit latitude/ longitude" permission to the *Anonymous User* role. This setting would be necessary if people need to submit their location when creating their user profile.

4. No changes are needed on the Location module configuration page at *admin/config/ content/location*.

5. The more important configuration page is the Geocoding options tab at *admin/ config/content/location/geocoding*. *Geocoding* is the process of turning some text (such as an address) into numerical spatial information (such as a latitude and longitude). It will be discussed in more detail below in "Geocoding" on page 41.

   The first field on the form sets how accurate we require geocoding to be. For our example, we are mapping the location of Drupal businesses, so it is quite important to know where these businesses are. However, people are not going to be using our maps to drive or walk to the location. To require a higher level of accuracy than the default, change the setting to "Town."

6. The second group of choices are which geocoding service to use for every country in the world. Not every country has a service that can geocode an address (e.g., North Korea doesn't), but for almost every country that does, Google is the only choice. Unfortunately you have to manually select Google Maps for each country, so do this for every country that you care about. For the United States and Australia you also have the choice of using Yahoo!'s geocoding service; for Canada there is the option of GeoCode.ca.

If you need to work with lots of countries, see the Note on page 39 for a simpler way to set up geocoding for the Location module.

7. After you click the "Save configuration" button, you will see a "Configure parameters" link next to each country for which you have enabled geocoding. Click on one of these links to bring up the form to enter the Google Maps API Key. Thankfully this API Key only needs to be entered once; it does not need to be repeated for each country. Go to the Google Maps API Sign Up (*http://code.google.com/apis/ maps/signup.html*) page to get the key.

8. Read the terms, particularly the usage limits, as these can have a significant implication for your website if you expect high traffic volumes or if you are using the maps on an intranet or other site that is not accessible for free by the public.

9. Tick the box and enter the URL for your site. It is best to enter the domain without the www (e.g., `http://mappingdrupal.com`). If you have a development or local ver-

sion of your site, this API key will work on subdomains of this URL (e.g., *http://staging.mappingdrupal.com* or *http://local.mappingdrupal.com*), but the API key will not work on other domains (e.g., *http://localhost/mappingdrupal* or *http://mappingwithdrupal.com*). You will need to sign up for a different API key for those other domains.

10. Copy your new API Key (the long string of letters and numbers) to the "Google Maps API Key" field on your site and click the "Save configuration" button.

Adding geographic data to a node with the Location module

Now that we have the necessary modules enabled and the Google Maps API key stored, we need to create the content type to store information about Drupal development companies. The content type will contain the company's name, a short description, and its address.

1. From the Content types page, add a new content type at *admin/structure/types/add*.

2. Enter **Drupal Company** as the Name.

3. Enter **A Drupal development company** as the Description.

4. Change the "Title field label" to **Company name**.

5. All other options can remain as default for now. Click the "Save and add fields" button.

6. You are now taken to the "Manage fields" page for this content type at *admin/structure/types/manage/drupal-company/fields*. The third field listed should be "Body." Click the "edit" link to change this.

7. Change the "Label" field to **Company description**. All other fields can stay with the default values. Click the "Save settings" button.

8. On the "Manage fields" page, go to the "Add new field" row. Enter **Company location** as the Label and **company_location** as the Field name. In the "Select a field type" drop-down, choose "Location." In the Widget drop-down, choose "Location Field."

9. Click the "Save" button at the bottom of the page to create this field.

10. The next screen that comes up is the Field settings for the Company location field. This determines both what information will be collected when someone creates a new Drupal company, and also what information will be displayed about that company when someone views the site.

11. Under "Collection settings", change the Collect drop-down for "Location name" to "Do not collect." We are using the title field for this information. Leave "Street location," "Additional," "Country," and "Coordinate Chooser" set at "Allow." Change "City," "State/Province," and "Postal code" to "Allow." There is also a field to set a default value for each of these fields, and to use the "Force Default" option to only allow users to enter an address for a particular country, state, etc.

12. The Display Settings section allows certain fields to be hidden. Leave these all visible for now. Click the "Save field settings" button.

13. On the final screen, tick the "Required field" checkbox so that a location has to be set for this content type. Click the "Save settings" button.

14. Create some "Drupal Company" content. From the "Add Content" page at *node/add*, add a "Drupal Company." Enter the name and description of a company, and a full street address. Click the "Save" button. You should now see something similar to Figure 3-5. If you do not see the address, check the modules page at *admin/modules* to make sure that you did not accidentally enable the Node Location module (see Warning on page 34).

Figure 3-5. A Drupal Company

15. It is useful to see the latitude and longitude below the address so that we know that geocoding has been successful, but we do not need to display this to people visiting our site. In this example we do not want to show the "See Map" link either. Go to the "Manage fields" page for the content type at *admin/structure/types/manage/drupal-company/fields/field_company_location* and edit the "Company location" field. At the very end of this form, under the "Display Settings" section, check the "Map link" and "Coordinates" checkboxes to prevent these from being displayed. Click the "Save settings" button to save your changes.

Extending the Location module with the GMap module

Seeing the address of a business is useful, but often you want to display a map of a business. The easiest way to do this with the Location module is to use the GMap module. Like the Location module, the GMap module has been around since Drupal 4.6 in 2005, and its architecture reflects that. It is a very large module, but it integrates well with the Location module and is in use on tens of thousands of sites. It implements various parts of the Google Maps API on Drupal sites. The GMap module does three specific things:

1. It provides a clickable map for entering the location of a node.

2. It provides a map to display a node's location.

3. It integrates with the Views module to display the results of a View on a Google map.

In this exercise we will cover the first two aspects of the module. The third aspect will be covered in "Mapping with the GMap Module" on page 60.

 The GMap module integrates with version two of the Google Maps JavaScript API (*http://code.google.com/apis/maps/documentation/java script/v2/*). This version of the API was deprecated in May 2010. While it will continue to work, it lacks the newer features of the current version three Google Maps JavaScript API (*http://code.google.com/apis/maps/ documentation/javascript/*), such as mobile support, better speed, and removing the need for an API key. There are plans in the module's issue queue (*http://drupal.org/node/818638*) to add support for version three, but this is a large task, so it is unlikely to happen soon. The GMap module works fine for most purposes despite this.

1. There is not yet a stable release of the GMap module (*http://drupal.org/project/ gmap*) for Drupal 7, but the development version works fine. Download the latest development release to your site's modules directory.

2. Enable two modules: the GMap and GMap Location modules at *admin/modules*. There are some permissions that can be set for these modules, but they apply to components that are not used by these examples.

 The GMap Location module is only used in these examples to allow different kinds of markers to be selected for different content types. This module also creates a page that displays a map of all content on your site, which is rarely useful. For many websites, this module will not be necessary and does not need to be enabled. The GMap module, however, should be used.

3. Go to the GMap configuration page at *admin/config/services/gmap*. You will get a JavaScript error about the Google Maps API Key. Click OK to dismiss this message, and enter the same API Key that you entered earlier when configuring the Location module in Step 10 on page 36. Leave all the other settings at their default value for now and scroll to the bottom of the page to click the "Save configuration" button.

The process of setting up the Google Maps API key earlier in "Basic configuration of location" on page 34 can actually be skipped because, when geocoding, the Location Module first tries to use the GMap module's API key. If the GMap module is not installed, the Location module falls back to its own API key. In the Location Module exercise, we did not skip that configuration because we were seeing how the Location module worked when the GMap module was not installed.

If your site will be accessed from several different domains, use the Keys module (*http://drupal.org/project/keys*) to automatically switch to the correct API key for each domain.

4. When the page reloads after saving, you should not get the JavaScript error, and you should see a small Google Map of southern Europe and northern Africa. If you do not see these things, check that you have entered the API Key correctly.

5. Go to the Location module's configuration page at *admin/config/content/location/main* and tick the "Use a Google Map to set latitude and longitude" checkbox. This will allow users to click on a map to set the business's location instead of (or in addition to) entering an address. Click the "Save configuration" button.

6. Create some more "Drupal Company" content. From the "Add Content" page at *node/add* add a "Drupal Company." Enter the name and description of a company. For this example, we will create a virtual company that does not have an office address, and instead has a PO Box like, "PO Box 23505, Brooklyn, NY 11202." This address, when geocoded by Google, shows up in downtown Brooklyn. To see this, click the "Save" button.

If you want to create lots of content for testing a new site, the Devel Generate module (*http://drupal.org/project/devel*) will do this for you. When doing this, the GMap module will insert random countries and coordinates for this content.

7. Edit the company that you just saved. On the small map, zoom in until you can see the streets. The business owner of this company wants to be associated with downtown Manhattan, so click the map in that location and notice how the latitude and longitude fields change. (There are two pairs of latitude and longitude: one showing the current coordinates for the node under the heading "Current Coordinates"; and the other pair, further down the form, appearing as two text fields. The latter are the ones that change when you click a new location on the map.) Click the "Save" button again. The business still has the same address, but if you edit the business again, you will see that the location on the map is now lower Manhattan, where you clicked, and the "Source" for the current coordinates is now "User-submitted" instead of "Geocoded (Exact)."

This is a useful feature when mapping things that cannot be easily geocoded, such as a park, or when you are mapping things at a very detailed scale and want to pinpoint the entrance to a conference hall rather than the middle of the building.

8. As you edit the business and look at the map, you have found it unhelpful because it is a small map showing most of the world. To change this, go to the Location module's configuration page again at *admin/config/content/location/main*. Toward the bottom of this page is a field titled "Location chooser macro," which contains [gmap]. This is the GMap module's way of setting up behaviors and display options for a map. The current setting uses the default values set on the GMap module's configuration page, *admin/config/services/gmap*. The easiest way to create a new macro is to use the module provided for this purpose.

9. Go to the module page at *admin/modules* and enable the GMap Macro Builder module. Enable permissions for the roles that will need to configure map defaults at *admin/people/permissions#module-gmap_macro_builder*—usually just the "Administrator role."

10. Go to the "Build a GMap macro" page at *map/macro*. The map at the top of this page is the one that will be set by the macro that you are creating. The first section is the "Overlay editor." When someone is editing a location, the Overlay editor determines stuff like the colors of the map pins and lines. The defaults are fine for now.

11. The next section of the form contains the more important settings. If you are creating a website that has a particular geographic focus, you probably want a map that defaults to a location in that area, rather than one that shows the whole world. Enter a location that represents this focus in the "Address" field (for example, New York, NY). When you click or tab out of this field, the location will be geocoded and the latitude and longitude will be updated below, in the field labeled "The Latitude and Longitude of the centre of the map."

12. If you scroll back to the top of the page, you will now see a small map centered on the location you entered. The map is still very zoomed out, so change this in the field labeled "The current magnification of the map." This defaults to 3, so increase it and look at the updated map at the top of the page to see if the new value works.

13. We now have the map showing a more useful location, but it is still very small. To change the size of the map, we need to update the "Map width" and "Map height" fields. For a map that is being used to set a location, we want to use the full space available on the page, so change the width to 95%. Percentage heights are not well supported across browsers, so change the height to 300px.

14. As you have gone through these steps, you may have noticed that the last field on the page, "Macro text," has been changing each time you changed a value. It should now read something like:

```
[gmap zoom=9 |center=40.7143528,-74.0059731 |width=95% |height=300px |
control=Small |type=Map]
```

Copy this macro (it can not be saved) and go back to the Location module's configuration page at *admin/config/content/location/main*. Paste the macro you created into the "Location chooser macro" field. Click the "Save configuration" button.

15. Now, if you create a new Drupal company, you will see that the map is much larger, it is showing at a more useful scale, and it is centered on the location that you set. If you edit an existing Drupal company, you will see that the map is centered on that company's location, but that the zoom level is the same as you set in the macro, and the width and height of the map are also as you set.

The GMap module has allowed for a richer user interface for adding location information. In Chapter 4 we will integrate this with the Views module, so as to display multiple locations on a map for people visiting the site.

Geocoding

In "Adding geographic data to a node with the Location module" on page 36 we introduced the concept of geocoding. Geocoding is the process of creating spatial data from nonspatial information. Geocoding can be converting an address into latitude and longitude coordinate, or turning the name "Mount Everest" into a polygon. Going in the opposite direction, turning geospatial data into nongeospatial data, such as a coordinate into an address, is called *reverse-geocoding*.

 The process of geocoding, especially address conversion, usually involves a large amount of data and heavy processing power. This means that you are unlikely to create your own geocoding service, and it is why most of these modules integrate with existing services.

Modules

We have already worked through an example where the Location module geocoded the address that you entered for the Drupal company content type. To achieve similar results for the Geofield module, we will use the Geocoder and Addressfield modules. One other module that handles geocoding for Drupal 7 is the Geonames module, which will be briefly discussed.

Geocoder and Addressfield

To integrate with the OpenLayers and Geofield modules, the easiest way to allow users to enter an address and have it automatically geocoded is to install the Addressfield and Geocoder modules. For our example website, we will create a new content type to store Drupal events. The content type will contain the name of the event, a description of the event, a date, an address, and a latitude and longitude.

Be careful not to confuse the Geocode and the Geocoder modules. They are two separate modules, though Geocoder is mostly a Drupal 7 port of Geocode, which is only for Drupal 6. There is a post in the Geocode issue queue (*http://drupal.org/node/982534*) that provides some background on the two modules and their future.

1. Download the latest stable release of the Addressfield module (*http://drupal.org/project/addressfield*) to your site's modules directory.
2. Enable the Address Field module at *admin/modules*. There are no configuration or permissions changes needed for this module.
3. From the "Content types page," add a new content type at *admin/structure/types/add*.
4. Enter **Event** as the Name.
5. For the Description, enter **A Drupal event.**
6. Change the "Title field label" to **Event name**.
7. All other options can remain as default for now. Click the "Save and add fields" button.
8. You are now taken to the "Manage fields" page for this content type at *admin/structure/types/manage/event/fields*. The third field listed should be "Body." Click the "edit" link to change this.
9. Change the "Label" field to **Event details**. All other fields can stay with the default values. Click the "Save settings" button.
10. On the "Manage fields" page, go to the "Add new field" row. Enter **Event location** as the Label and **event_location** as the Field name. In the "Select a field type" drop-down, choose "Postal address." In the Widget drop-down, choose "Dynamic address form" (the only choice).
11. Click the "Save" button at the bottom of the page to create this field.
12. On the screen that comes up there are no further field settings, so click the "Save field settings" button.
13. The final configuration page for this field is where the field is configured for the Event content type at *admin/structure/types/manage/event/fields/field_event_location*. Set it to be a required field by checking the "Required field" checkbox.
14. Under the "Available countries" field, to enable all countries leave it at the default with nothing selected, or else select a few countries.
15. The "Format handlers" checkboxes allow different fields to be shown in addition to the default country-specific address form. For example, if you are using the address for shipping a product to customers, you might want to enable the Name and Organization fields. In this example just leave it as the default "Address form."

16. It is possible to set a default value for the address or to allow multiple addresses (for example, for different invoicing and shipping addresses), but in this example just leave all the values unchanged.

17. Click the "Save settings" button.

We have now created a content type for an event with a title, a description and an address.

How does this differ from the address field provided by the Location module in "Adding geographic data to a node with the Location module" on page 36? If you are building a website that will be used outside the United States, the differences are significant.

1. Create some "Event" content at *node/add/event*. Enter the name and description of an event. Try changing the country in the drop-down and see how the address form changes. For the United States, there is a drop-down field labeled "State" and a field labeled "ZIP Code." For Canada, the state field becomes "Province" and the ZIP Code becomes "Postal Code." The United Kingdom has the same "Postal Code" field but the "State" field is a text field rather than a drop-down. The United States and Canada are the only countries with a list of states or provinces included with the Addressfield module.

2. For comparison, create some "Drupal company" content at *node/add/drupal-company*. With the United States as the country, start typing the name of a state and notice how it autocompletes. Most countries have states or provinces that will autocomplete like this. However notice how the labels of the fields do not change; it is always "State/Province" and "Postal Code."

3. This comparison shows an important difference between the two approaches (Location and GMap versus Geofield and Addressfield). Location and GMap give you more functionality just by installing the modules. OpenLayers, Geofield, and Addressfield give you less ready-made functionality, but they try to be more semantically correct with the data, and they provide a pluggable API to add the data that you need. For example, if there is a country for which you need a list of states, you can look at the addressfield_example module that is included inside the Addressfield module to see how to do this (the example shows how to add states for Switzerland).

The Event content type that we have created has an address, but this is not yet being geocoded. The Geocoder module will integrate with the Geofield and Address modules to handle this.

1. Download the latest release of the Geocoder module (*http://drupal.org/project/geocoder*) to your site's modules directory. At the time of writing there is no stable release, so download the latest development release.

2. Enable the Geocoder API module. There are no configuration or permissions changes needed for this module.

3. On the "Manage fields" page for the Event content type at *admin/structure/types/manage/event/fields* go to the "Add new field" row. Enter **Event geo** as the Label and **event_geo** as the Field name. In the "Select a field type" drop-down, choose "Geofield." In the Widget drop-down, choose "Geocode from another field."

4. Click the "Save button" at the bottom of the page to create this field.

5. On the next screen that comes up, there are no further field settings, so click the "Save field settings" button.

6. This field will never be visible to a user of your website when they are creating events, so many of the settings on the final configuration page at *admin/structure/types/manage/event/fields/field_event_geo* are unnecessary. There are two important fields, though.

7. Under "Geocode from field," select "Event location" (the field that contains the address).

> The Geocoder module can geocode any text field that contains properly formatted location data. It can also get the location from an uploaded JPEG photo that contains a geotag embedded as EXIF in the metadata. Many recent digital cameras and smartphones support this.

8. Under the "Geocoder" drop-down, select "Google Geocoder."

9. Click the "Save settings" button.

10. The final step is to set the display for this field. Rather than displaying the latitude and longitude, the location of the event should be displayed on a map. Go to the "Manage Display" page for the Event content type at *admin/structure/types/manage/event/display*. For the "Event geo" field, change the Label to "<Hidden>". Change the Format to "OpenLayers." Click on the cog on the right side to configure the "OpenLayers display" widget. In the "OpenLayers Preset" drop-down, select "Geofield Formatter Map." In the "Data options" drop-down, choose "Use full geometry."

> The "Geofield Formatter Map" is the default map display that comes with the Geofield module. As shown in Figure 3-6, this default map is quite small-scale (zoomed out). If you wish to change this, you can create a new map preset, as described in "Setting Up an OpenLayers Map" on page 48. Including the Geofield placeholder layer in a new preset will make it show up in the list in the "OpenLayers Preset" drop-down.

11. Click the "Update" button to save the field display widget, and then click the "Save" button to save all the display settings.

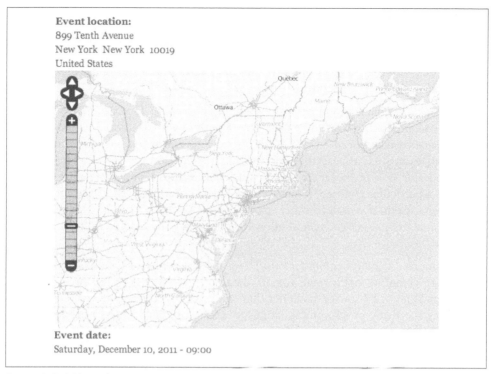

Event location:
899 Tenth Avenue
New York New York 10019
United States

Event date:
Saturday, December 10, 2011 - 09:00

Figure 3-6. A Drupal Event

The Event content type now displays a map with the geocoded location of the event, but is missing the crucial thing for an event: the date.

1. Download the latest release of the Date module (*http://drupal.org/project/date*) to your site's modules directory.
2. Enable the Date, Date API, and Date Popup modules. There are no important permissions or other configuration changes needed for these modules.
3. Go back to the "Manage fields" page for the Event content type at *admin/structure/types/manage/event/fields* and go to the "Add new field" row. Enter **Event date** as the Label and **event_date** as the Field name. In the "Select field" drop-down, choose "Date." In the Widget drop-down, choose "Pop-up calendar."
4. Click the "Save button" at the bottom of the page to create this field.
5. The default field settings should be fine, so just click the "Save field settings" button. The default values on the next page are fine too, so click "Save settings."

Create a new Event. Include an address and a date using the "Event date" field. When you save the Event, the address should be geocoded and displayed on the map as shown in Figure 3-6.

Other geocoding modules and services

The Location and Geocoder modules for Drupal 7 are the only ones that will geocode addresses entered by users. However, there are some other geocoding services that can be integrated with Drupal if you are able to do some coding: among them are GeoNames and the GeoCommons Geocoder.

GeoNames (*http://www.geonames.org/*) is a huge geographic database that is available to download and use for free under a Creative Commons Attribution 3.0 License (*http://creativecommons.org/licenses/by/3.0/*). It provides several services for looking up spatial information, such as searching for location information for place names, finding postal codes or Wikipedia articles near a particular location, or getting a list of postal codes for a particular country. It does not provide a geocoding service for an address, but it is very useful if you need other structured spatial data. The GeoNames module (*http://drupal.org/project/geonames*) allows you to query these services from a Drupal site.

GeoCommons (*http://geocommons.com/*) is a mapping platform and a community working to create an open repository of data and maps. One of the projects being worked on is an open source geocoder that can be installed on your own server. It is built using the Ruby programming language, and it currently only works for US addresses because it is based on the US Census Bureau's free TIGER/Line data set. It can be downloaded from the GeoCommons github page (*https://github.com/geocommons/geocoder*). Installing this and configuring it to work with a Drupal site is a significant effort, but if you need to geocode large amounts of US-based addresses and cannot use one of the web-based geocoding services because of license restrictions, this is a good alternative.

CHAPTER 4

Displaying Maps

Few Drupal sites are built without the Views module (*http://drupal.org/project/views*), and Views underlies much of the mapping in Drupal. This chapter explores different ways of displaying spatial data, primarily through the Google and OpenLayers Java-Script mapping APIs, but also using lists, tables, and data feeds.

There are two main choices for displaying maps in Drupal: the OpenLayers JavaScript library and the GMap module's implementation of the Google Maps API. This chapter covers how to create maps with both modules.

The GMap module is the more straightforward to understand. It contains code to pull data from your Drupal website and display it on a Google Map. Continuing our earlier example, this will be a map of Drupal companies.

The OpenLayers module for Drupal does a similar thing, but it uses a different Java-Script API to display the map, and it allows you to choose from several different base tile sets, including sets from Google Maps, OpenStreetMap, Bing, and more. Continuing our earlier example, this will be a map of Drupal user groups.

Mapping with the OpenLayers Module

OpenLayers (*http://openlayers.org/*) is a JavaScript library for displaying maps. It is a free, open source project, which means that you can use the maps you create in any way that you want and that, if you're so inclined, you can help improve the code. At the most basic level, the OpenLayers module allows maps to be displayed on a Drupal website. The module provides a way to configure the appearance of maps and to choose *behaviors* for the maps. The display of the data on the map is done by integrating with the Views module. Each of these steps is outlined below.

Basic Configuration of OpenLayers

1. Download the latest release of the OpenLayers module (*http://drupal.org/project/openlayers*) for Drupal 7 to your site's contributed modules directory. You will also

need the Chaos Tools module (*http://drupal.org/project/ctools*) and the Views module (*http://drupal.org/project/views*), as they are required by OpenLayers.

2. Enable all three modules that come with OpenLayers (Figure 4-1). The OpenLayers UI module provides a user interface for configuring your maps and can be disabled once work is complete on your site. The OpenLayers Views module integrates OpenLayers with the Views module. The Chaos Tools module, Views module, and Views UI module must also be enabled.

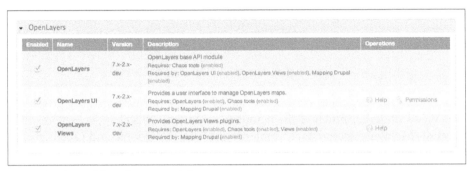

Figure 4-1. List of OpenLayers modules

3. Configure permissions for OpenLayers by following the "Permissions" link on the Modules page, or by going directly to the Permissions page at *admin/people/permissions*. There is only one permission, "Administer OpenLayers," which should only be given to trusted administrators. You do not want normal users of your site to change the appearance and behavior of the maps on your site.

Setting Up an OpenLayers Map

In the OpenLayers module, a map is a combination of three things: *layers* of data (such as map tiles or markers), *styles* that are applied to some of these layers, and *behaviors* (interactions that are attached to maps). OpenLayers uses the Views module in two ways: first to create data layers to display on the map, as a map is a set of layers, and second to display the final map as a block or page. We start this exercise by creating a layer using Views, and then will use Views again to create the final map.

This is the place where most users get confused with the OpenLayers module, and rightfully so. The module uses Views *twice*. This means that you will have to go to the Views interface, back to the OpenLayers interface, and back to Views. The goal is to change this in future versions of the OpenLayers module so that the user experience is more intuitive.

OpenLayers layers

Layers can be put into two categories. The *base layer* contains the underlying map, which is usually the tile set, such as MapQuest's Open Aerial tiles; there is only one of these displayed at a time. The *overlay layers* contain all your added data, such as icons marking businesses, compost facilities, or public toilets; there can be multiple overlay layers displayed on one map. The base layer can be thought of as the map layer; the overlay layer can be thought of as the data layer.

The OpenLayers module comes with several map layers, including four types of Google map tiles (normal, satellite, hybrid, and physical), three types of Yahoo! map tiles (satellite, street, and hybrid), three types of Bing map tiles (satellite, street, and hybrid), and four types of OpenStreetMap tiles. You can see these on the Layers Configuration page at *admin/structure/openlayers/layers*. Other Drupal modules, such as MapBox, add even more map layers. Adding further map layers is discussed in Chapter 6. For the examples in this chapter we are just going to use one of the default map layers.

The data overlays are more critical to understand because this is where you will be able to add your Drupal data and then put it on a map. By utilizing Views, you can create many data overlays to go on a single map. Data overlays can also come from an external source, such as a KML file, but this is managed through the OpenLayers Layers interface.

To summarize, there are four stages in creating a map using the OpenLayers module:

1. Create a data layer to receive the user-supplied data about Drupal groups.
2. Create a Map to display this data layer over a map layer.
3. Create a page to display your Map.
4. Tweak the Styles and Behaviors to beautify how your data appears on your Map.

The most common way to create a data layer is using the Views module. In "Geofield Module" on page 29 we created some Drupal user groups. We will use Views and OpenLayers to display all of these on a map.

1. From the Views page add a new view, *admin/structure/views/add*.
2. For the "View name," enter **Drupal groups**.
3. Tick the "Description" checkbox and enter this description: **Drupal groups data layer for a map**. This description will show up later in the user interface and is helpful there.
4. In the "Show" section, leave "Content" selected from the first drop-down. Change the "type" drop-down to "User Group." Leave the "sorted by" drop-down set to "Newest first."

 If you do not see the "User Group," make sure that you created this content type in "Geofield Module" on page 29.

5. Uncheck the "Create a page" checkbox. At this stage we are creating a data layer, not a page or block.

6. Click the "Continue & edit" button.

7. Click the "Add" button (circled in red in Figure 4-2) and click on "OpenLayers Data Overlay" from the list of *displays* that shows.

Figure 4-2. Adding a display to a View

8. Enter a Title for the View, such as `Drupal groups data layer`.

 The Views module allows you to create multiple *displays* in one View. In this example we are only creating an "OpenLayers Data Overlay" display. Other displays include a Page, Block, or Feed. If you have multiple displays in one view, you need to be aware of whether you are changing a setting for one display or all displays. For simplicity, we will only have one display in this View, so for this and all following settings the changes that you make can be applied to all displays.

9. In the "Fields" section of the Views configuration form we need to add the fields that contain the location information for our "User Group" content type. This is the information that OpenLayers is going to extract from our stored data, interpret, and use to display the data layer of our map. Click the "add" button (circled in red in Figure 4-3).

10. On the list of fields that shows, find the field labelled "Content: Group location" and select it, then click the "Add and configure fields" button, shown in Figure 4-4.

11. On the "Configure field" screen that comes up next, untick the "Create a label" option. Tick "Exclude from display." All other settings can stay the same. Click the "Apply (all displays)" button to save the configuration.

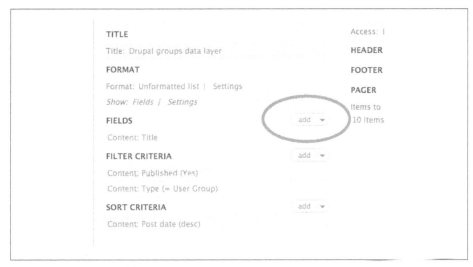

Figure 4-3. Adding a field to a display

Figure 4-4. Adding the Group location field

12. Back on the "OpenLayers Data Overlay details" screen we need another field. This time, add the "Content: Body" field. This one will contain the user-supplied descriptions of all our Drupal user groups. Click the "Apply (all displays)" button to save the configuration.

13. By adding these fields, we now have all the data necessary to create our data layer, but OpenLayers does not yet know which of these fields contain the spatial data and which fields are merely descriptive.

    Back on the "OpenLayers Data Overlay details" screen under the "Format" heading, click on the "Unformatted list" link (circled in red in Figure 4-5). Select the only radio button available, "OpenLayers Data Overlay," and click the "Apply (all displays)" button to save.

14. On the Style options screen that loads next, change the "Map Data Sources" drop-down to WKT. In the "WKT Field" that appears below, select the field that contains the WKT value, "Group location." In "Title Field," choose "Title" in the drop-

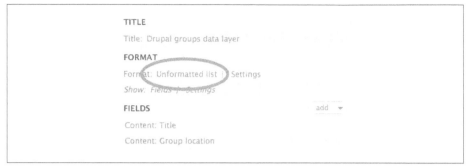

| TITLE |
| Title: Drupal groups data layer |
| FORMAT |
Format: Unformatted list	Settings
Show: Fields	Settings
FIELDS	add ▾
Content: Title
Content: Group location

Figure 4-5. Changing the display format

down. In "Description Field," select "Body." Click the "Apply (all displays)" button to save.

15. Back on the "OpenLayers Data Overlay details" screen again, one last setting to change is the *pager*. The Views module is normally used to create lists of content, such as "my 10 most recent blog posts." The pager is used there to let people read through all the older blog posts. For our map, we want to show more than 10 places. Under "Items to display," click the "10 items" link. On the screen that loads, change "Items to display" to **100**. Click the "Apply (all displays)" button to save.

 See "Browser Capabilities" on page 22 on why to avoid displaying an unlimited amount of data.

16. The View that creates the data layer for the map is now complete. Click the "Save" button on the top right.

There is now a data layer—but as yet, no underlying map! So now, finally, we must choose some mapping to form our map (base) layer and combine it with our data layer to form a Drupal "Map."

OpenLayers Maps

The next step is to create what the OpenLayers module refers to as a "Map." To distinguish this from all the other things referred to as maps, however, we will refer to it as a "Map Configuration," because this is where we will define the combinations of layers, styles, and behaviors that constitute a map. On the OpenLayers Maps page at *admin/structure/openlayers/maps* there are several default Map Configurations: one that comes with the OpenLayers module, and two that are added by the Geofield module. We will create a new Map Configuration to display our "Drupal user group" data layer.

In OpenLayers in Drupal 6, Map Configurations were called "presets."

1. Add a new Map Configuration at *admin/structure/openlayers/maps/add*.

2. Enter a name for this Map Configuration. It will be used internally by Drupal to store the Map Configuration, so it should be lowercase characters, numbers, or underscores (e.g., **user_groups**).

3. Enter a title and a description for this Map Configuration. These will be seen by you in other parts of the user interface, so make them descriptive (e.g., **Drupal user groups** and **A map of Drupal user groups around the world**).

4. Most of the other values in this "General information" tab should remain with the default values, though change the Height to **500px**. It is often useful to leave the width at **auto**; this will make the map fill the full width of the page. We will cover the use of the "Image Path" and "CSS Path" in "The Map Interface" on page 103.

5. Before clicking the "Save" button, take a look at the configuration options in the other tabs on this page. First click on "Center & Bounds."

6. The "Center & Bounds" tab contains the defaults for the centerpoint and zoom level for the map, and provides a map interface to change these values. Leave these at the default values for now.

7. The "Layers & Styles" tab is where OpenLayers pulls in the data layer that was created in "OpenLayers layers" on page 48. The "Map Projection" and "Display Projection" sections can be left unchanged. From the list of "Base layers" (the map layers), choose "OSM Mapnik" as the default and tick the "Enabled" checkbox.

8. Still in the "Layers & Styles" tab, go to the "Overlay layers" table. Tick the "Enabled" and "Activated" checkboxes for your "Drupal groups data layer" layer.

 You set the title of the "Drupal groups data layer" in Step 8 on page 50.

9. Finally, click on the "Behaviors" tab. This configures the interactive elements of the map. We will discuss the various behaviors in more detail in "Exploring OpenLayers Behaviors" on page 57, but for now just tick the Attribution, Popup, Navigation, and PanZoomBar checkboxes. When you click the Popup checkbox, an option will open below to select which layer will contain the data for the pop ups. Here, tick the box labelled "drupal_groups_openlayers_1," as this is the data layer that was enabled in the previous step.

You may have to save the Map Configuration before the "drupal_groups_openlayers_1" option shows under the Popup behavior. This is because the interface is not AJAX-enabled and does not know yet that you have enabled that layer.

10. Click the "Save" button to save your Map Configuration. It will now show in the list of OpenLayers maps at *admin/structure/openlayers/maps*.

We now have a Map Configuration and need a way to display the map on a page of the website.

Using Views to display an OpenLayers map

The simplest way to display an OpenLayers map uses the Views module. The View creates a page that uses the Map Configuration from the previous step .

1. Add a new View at *admin/structure/views/add*.
2. For the "View name," enter **Map of Drupal groups**.
3. Leave the "Create a page" checkbox ticked, and leave the default Page title and Path.
4. Change the first "Display format" drop-down to "OpenLayers Map".
5. Click the "Continue & edit" button.
6. On the "Page details" configuration page, under "Format" (circled in red in Figure 4-6), click on the "Settings" link.

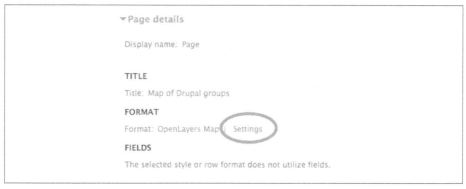

Figure 4-6. Changing the map display

7. In the "Map" drop-down, select "Drupal user groups." Click the "Apply (all displays)" button to save.
8. Click the "Save" button on the top right to save the view and create the map display.
9. On the right of the page is a "view page" button. Click this to view the map. It should look something like Figure 4-7. You can see an example of this online (*http://mappingdrupal.com/map-of-drupal-groups*).

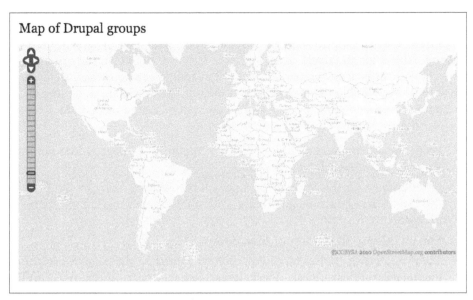

Figure 4-7. Completed map of Drupal user groups

10. If you click on the marker for one of the Drupal user groups, you will see a pop up open with the name of the group and its description. If the person adding the information has entered a long description, the pop up will be really wide and might go off the edge of the map, as shown in Figure 4-8. If you want a long description, it is possible to make the pop up narrower using CSS. Alternatively, the description can be truncated in the View configuration. Edit the view that contains the data layer at *admin/structure/views/view/drupal_groups/edit*. Under the "Fields" section, click on "Content: Body (Body)." Expand the "Rewrite results" section. Tick the "Trim this field to a maximum length" checkbox. In the "Maximum length," enter **60** (which will be 60 characters). Leave all other options as their defaults. Click the "Apply (all displays)" button to save. Click the "Save" button on the top right again.

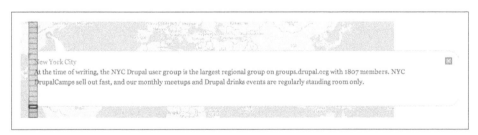

Figure 4-8. Oversized pop up

We now have a map that displays Drupal user groups, but an orange dot on the map isn't a particularly inspiring representation of a Drupal group. The next section will allow customization of styles on the map.

OpenLayers styles

OpenLayers styles provide a way to determine the appearance of geographic data: for example, the color and thickness of lines, the radius of points, or the opacity of polygons. Styles can be icons or markers, as well as simple geometric shapes like a circle. The OpenLayers module comes with some default styles, which can be seen at *admin/structure/openlayers/styles*. We will add a new style of dot to display the Drupal user groups that are being displayed on our map.

1. From the OpenLayers module's "Styles configuration" page, add a new Style at *admin/structure/openlayers/styles/add*.

2. Enter a name for this Style. The name will be used internally by Drupal to store this Style, so should be lowercase with underscores instead of spaces (e.g., **blue_dots**).

3. Enter a title for this Style (e.g., **Blue dots**).

4. There are lots of choices for Styles, each explained on the page. Most can be left unchanged for this example. The first one to change is "pointRadius." Our Drupal user groups show as points on the map, so we need to set the size in pixels for the point. Set it to **5**.

5. "fillColor" is the hexadecimal value of the color that will fill the circle where there is a Drupal user group. Enter **#53b0eb**, which is the shade of blue used commonly in Drupal's branding.

6. "strokeColor" is the color of the line surrounding the circle. Enter **#0678be**, a darker blue.

7. "strokeWidth" is the thickness of the line surrounding the circle. Leave this at **1**.

8. "fillOpacity" determines if the circle that represents the user group location is transparent or opaque. The default value of 1 means that it is opaque. Change this to **0.8** to make it slightly transparent.

9. "strokeOpacity" determines the opacity or transparency of the line surrounding the circle. Leave this at **1**.

10. Save this new Style. It will show in the list of OpenLayers styles at *admin/structure/openlayers/styles*.

To use this Style on the map of Drupal user groups, we need to update the Map Configuration from "OpenLayers Maps" on page 52.

1. From the OpenLayers module's maps page at *admin/structure/openlayers/maps*, click the edit link for the "Drupal user groups" map.

2. Click on the "Layers & Styles" tab.

3. In the "Overlay Layers" table, find the "Drupal groups data layer." Change the Style drop-down to the "Blue dots" style that you just created.

4. Click the "Save" button.

5. View your map again. You should see a blue dot instead of the orange dot. If you click on the marker, it will switch back to orange. This is because there are three states for a marker:

Default style
> What you see when the map loads

Select style
> What you see when you click on a marker

Temporary style
> What you see when adding a new marker to a map

6. To change the Select style for this map, edit the "Drupal user groups" Map Configuration again at *admin/structure/openlayers/maps/user_groups/edit* and go back to the "Layers & Styles" tab. At the very bottom of the page is the "Select style" drop-down. Change this to "Blue dots." You could also create a new Style and use it here instead.

You have now used the Geofield, OpenLayers, and Views modules to create a map that displays Drupal user groups around the world. The Style of the points of the map has been customized to be more appropriate than the default colors. The configuration of fields has been tidied up so that the pop ups do not fall off the edge of the map.

Exploring OpenLayers Behaviors

We have already explored some behaviors: in "OpenLayers Maps" on page 52 four *Behaviors* were chosen while setting up the Map Configuration. Behaviors in Open-Layers are map interactions such as pop ups, zoom controls, editing, and viewing full-screen. They can be added via the user interface in Drupal and can be extended by other modules.

 Behaviors are a concept for how to use JavaScript in Drupal that has been best practice since Drupal 6. More details can be found on the JavaScript handbook page (*http://drupal.org/node/756722*).

The OpenLayers Behaviors are all described on the Map Configuration page. Edit the User groups map that was created earlier at *admin/structure/openlayers/maps/user_groups/edit* and click on the "Behaviors" tab. There are lots of really useful Behaviors that come with the OpenLayers module, too many to describe here. Explore all the different Behaviors on your map and see how they work. Some of the most useful ones include:

Tooltip
> This can be used to display the title of a node when someone moves their mouse over a marker on a map.

Fullscreen

This provides a button that expands the map to the full size of the user's browser.

Layer Switcher

Using Views, you can create several layers that show different but related information. When configuring the map, you can enable several such data layers, and several base layers (e.g., a Bing street map and a Google Satellite map). All of these layers will be controlled by a layer-switching widget, and users can turn them on and off.

Cluster

See "Browser Capabilities" on page 22 for a description and rationale for clustering. OpenLayers comes with its own JavaScript clustering script. The OpenLayers examples site (*http://openlayers.org/dev/examples/strategy-cluster-threshold.html*) provides a good demonstration of how to configure this Behavior.

Geolocate

The latest version of the OpenLayers library takes advantage of HTML5 geolocation, as supported by most modern browsers, especially on smartphones and tablets. Users are prompted to allow the web page to access their location; then the map is updated to center on that location. A demonstration is on the OpenLayers examples site (*http://openlayers.org/dev/examples/geolocation.html*). This Behavior was added in version 2.11 of OpenLayers, so if you see the warning, "Dependency not found: OpenLayers.Control.Geolocate," this is because you are using an older version of the OpenLayers JavaScript library. That can be changed at *admin/structure/openlayers*.

Creating custom Behaviors is covered in Chapter 5.

Advanced OpenLayers Configuration

On the OpenLayers configuration page at *admin/structure/openlayers* you may have noticed a setting for where the *OpenLayers.js* file is located. By default the OpenLayers module will use a JavaScript file hosted on openlayers.org (*http://openlayers.org/api/2 .10/OpenLayers.js*). This works, but in most cases it is better to host the file yourself both for speed and reliability.

1. Download the latest stable release of the OpenLayers JavaScript library from openlayers.org (*http://openlayers.org*). Alternatively, you can check out the code from the OpenLayers subversion repository (*http://trac.osgeo.org/openlayers/wiki/ HowToDownload*).

2. Extract the *.zip* or *.tar.gz* file to your Drupal site, typically to a libraries directory inside the site's folder.

3. Update the OpenLayers configuration in your website at *admin/structure/openlayers* with the new location of the OpenLayers JavaScript file:
   `sites/all/libraries/OpenLayers-2.10/OpenLayers.js`.

While doing the steps above, you may have noticed that the OpenLayers JavaScript library is huge, and the *OpenLayers.js* file that is loaded to display a map is almost 1 MB. Once you have finished building all of your maps for a site, you can recompile this file to exclude all the Behaviors that are not needed. The library that you downloaded from *http://openlayers.org/* contains a Python script and instructions inside the build directory. Further instructions are in the OpenLayers module in *docs/CUSTOMIZATION.txt*.

Creating an OpenLayers Map Layer from KML

In "OpenLayers layers" on page 48 a data layer was created using the Views module. An alternative is to use a static KML file to create the data layer. KML was introduced in "Data Types" on page 17. Using a KML file to generate the data layer will usually be faster than using the Views module because the spatial data does not need to be queried from the database.

Find a KML file that you would like to display on your map; for example the USGS list of the world's largest earthquakes (*http://earthquake.usgs.gov/earthquakes/world/LargestWorldEarthquakes.kml*). Download this file and add it to your site. In this example, we've put it inside a custom module called "mappingdrupalexercises." Because this file will be loaded through JavaScript, most web browsers will block the file if it is not on the same website as the map that you are creating.

1. From the OpenLayers module's layers configuration page, add a new layer at *admin/structure/openlayers/layers/add*.
2. Click on KML in the list of layer types.
3. Enter the path of the KML file as the URL:
   `sites/all/modules/custom/mappingdrupalexercises/LargestWorldEarthquakes.kml`
4. Enter an ID for this layer (for example, **usgs_earthquakes**).
5. Enter a title and description, then save your new KML layer. It should show up on the list of layers at *admin/structure/openlayers/layers*.
6. Follow the instructions in "OpenLayers Maps" on page 52 to create a new Map Configuration, choosing your earthquake layer in the "Layers & Styles" tab.
7. Follow the instructions in "Using Views to display an OpenLayers map" on page 54 to display the map, choosing the Map Configuration that you just created.
8. You should end up with a map that looks something like Figure 4-9.

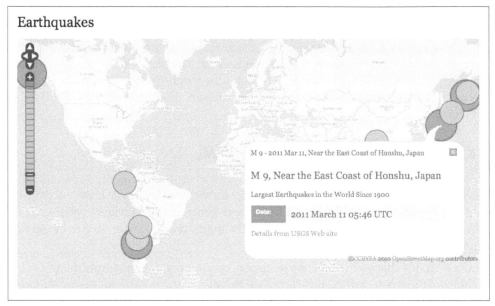

Figure 4-9. Earthquakes map

Mapping with the GMap Module

The GMap module integrates Drupal with the Google Maps API to display maps. One of its strengths is that it is faster and simpler than using the OpenLayers API to display Google Maps. The drawback is that you are then committed to using just Google Maps. Switching to another source would require big changes to your code and data. Google Maps are not open source; they come with restrictions. However, for many purposes they are free to use.

 If you are going to build a site that relies on Google Maps, it is worth reading and understanding the usage limits (*http://code.google.com/apis/ maps/faq.html#usagelimits*) and terms of service (*http://code.google .com/apis/maps/terms.html*).

Basic Configuration

The basic configuration of the GMap module was covered in "Extending the Location module with the GMap module" on page 37, so if you have been following through the examples, this module should already be installed and enabled.

Integrating with Views

Unlike the OpenLayers module, GMap does not require two separate displays, so creating a map is a little simpler. Just as it was when using the OpenLayers module, the maps are created using the Views module. In this example, we will use the GMap and Views modules to create a map of "Drupal companies." We created the "Drupal companies" content type earlier in "Adding geographic data to a node with the Location module" on page 36.

1. Download and install the Views module (*http://drupal.org/project/views*), including the Views UI module if you do not already have these set up for your site.

2. From the Views page, add a new view at *admin/structure/views/add*.

3. For the "View name," enter **Drupal companies**.

4. Tick the "Description" checkbox and enter the description **Map of Drupal companies**.

5. In the "Show" section, from the first drop down leave "Content" selected. Change the "type" drop-down to "Drupal Company." Leave the "sorted by" drop-down set to "Newest first."

 If you do not see the "Drupal Company" item in the drop-down, make sure that you created this content type in "Adding geographic data to a node with the Location module" on page 36.

6. Leave "Create a page" checked. This is the page that will contain the map. In the "Display format" section, change the first drop-down to "GMap." Change the second drop-down to "fields." Change "Items to display" to **100**.

 See "Browser Capabilities" on page 22 on why to avoid displaying an unlimited amount of data.

7. Click the "Continue & edit" button.

8. All the basic configuration has been done to create a map. Click the "Save" button on the top right.

9. Click the "view page" button on the right to see the map, which will be at */drupal-companies*. As shown in Figure 4-10, the default map is very small and shows an unhelpful part of the world, unless your Drupal companies are in southern Europe and northern Africa. If you drag the map around, you should see the locations that you added to the map.

10. Edit the view again. In the "Format" section, click the "Settings" link next to "Format: GMap" as shown in Figure 4-11.

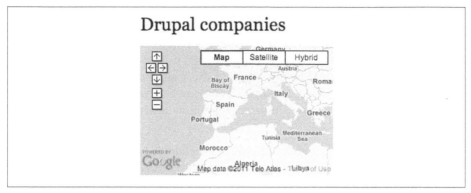

Figure 4-10. Basic map with GMap and Views

Figure 4-11. Configuring GMap in Views

11. The reason the map is small and centered on Spain is because of the *macro* that is being used for this View, which is currently set to **[gmap]**. The concept of a macro in the GMap module was introduced in "Extending the Location module with the GMap module" on page 37. Using the instructions from there, create a macro that will make the map fill the width of the page. It should be something like:

```
[gmap zoom=2 |center=27.9944,4.9218 |width=100% |height=400px |control=Small |
type=Map]
```

Enter this value into the "Macro" field on the Style options screen for the map view.

12. The next field is "Data source." For this example, it should be left set to "Location.module," but it is possible to change this if you need to select specific fields that contain the latitude and longitude. This makes it possible to use the GMap module in conjunction with the Geofield module, or with a content type that has latitude and longitude fields added in some other way.

13. The "Marker handling" field gives some options to choose which markers will be used on the map. For this example it could be left with the default "Use single marker type." The other options provide ways to have different markers representing different information on the map:

    By content type
    > To use markers by content type, configure the markers at *admin/config/services/gmap_location*. When configuring a location field for a content type at *admin/structure/types/manage/drupal-company/fields/field_company_location*, a particular style of marker can be chosen. This marker will then be used when a node of that content type is displayed on a map.

    Use marker field
    > This advanced configuration requires a field on a content type that matches the *markername* of a marker. The markernames can be found in the *.ini* files contained in the markers folder inside the GMap module.

14. With "Use single marker type" selected, the "Marker / fallback marker to use" field defaults to "Drupal." Change this to whatever marker you like, such as "Small Light Gray."

15. There are some more advanced choices on this form, but the last two checkboxes provide some useful Behaviors that can occur when people interact with the map. Tick the "Display a tooltip when hovering over markers" checkbox and select "Content: Title" to have the company name show when the user moves their mouse over a marker. Tick the "Display a popup bubble with additional information when a marker is clicked" checkbox and select "Content: Title" to have the company name show when a user clicks on a marker.

16. Click the "Apply (all displays)" button to save the configuration.

17. The view that creates the map is now complete. Click the "Save" button on the top right. The map should look something like Figure 4-12.

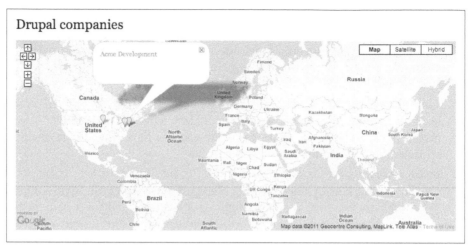

Figure 4-12. The final map of Drupal companies

18. Having the same information show up both on hover and in the pop up bubble is not very useful. We can improve this by adding a second field to the view so as to display the body of the node (the description of the Drupal company).

19. Edit the map view again. In the "Fields" section, click the "add" button. Select "Content: Body" from the list of available fields and click "Add and configure fields." Click the "Apply (all displays)" button to save the configuration.

20. Go back to the GMap settings for the view, as described in Step 10 on page 61. Change the "Bubble pop-up field" drop-down to "Content: Body." Click the "Apply (all displays)" button to save the configuration. Click the "Save" button on the top right to save these changes to the map. Clicking on a marker on the map should now display a more useful pop up bubble, as shown in Figure 4-13.

Figure 4-13. Pop up bubble with GMap

We have now used GMap and Views to create a map that displays all content of a particular type (Drupal businesses) with customized markers and useful information when hovering or clicking on a marker.

Other Ways of Displaying Spatial Data

Sometimes a map is not the most useful way to display spatial data. You may want to present information as a list, either on its own or alongside the same data on a map. Or it may be necessary to create an external feed so that your data can be pulled out into another service, such as Google Earth or a different website. Because maps made in Drupal are generally built using the Views module, it is a fairly simple process to output data in other formats.

Spatial Data in Tables and Lists

Foursquare on a mobile device is an example where it is more useful to have a list of nearby venues such as cafes, parks, or airports. Continuing with our example of upcoming Drupal events, it may be useful to see a list of events sorted by date, rather than a map of all of them. With the Views module, both of these are just *List* Views of the Map Views that we created earlier.

1. On the Views page, add a new View.
2. For the "View name," enter **Upcoming events**.
3. Enter a description of **A table of upcoming events**.
4. In the "Show" section, leave "Content" selected from the first drop-down. Change the "type" drop-down to "Event." Change the "sorted by" drop-down to "Unsorted."
5. Leave "Create a page" checked. This is the page that will contain the table of events. In the "Display format" section, change the first drop-down to "Table." Change "Items to display" to **100**.
6. Click the "Continue & edit" button.
7. In the "Fields" section, click the "add" button. From the list of available fields, select "Content: Event date" and click "Add and configure fields." In the "Choose how users view dates and times" field, select the "Medium" format. You could create custom date formats using the link below that field, but this is not necessary. Click the "Apply (all displays)" button.
8. In the "Fields" section, click the "add" button. Select "Content: Event location" from the list of available fields and click "Add and configure fields." Click the "Apply (all displays)" button.
9. In the "Fields" section, click the "add" button. Select "Content: Body" from the list of available fields and click "Add and configure fields." Change the "Label" field to **Description**. Expand the "Rewrite Results" section. Tick the "Trim this field to a maximum length" checkbox. Enter **100** as the maximum length. Leave the "Trim only on a word boundary" and "Add an ellipsis" checkboxes ticked. Again, click the "Apply (all displays)" button.

10. Below the view configuration form is a preview of the table that you are creating. The header of the table displays the field labels, but the header for the event name is missing. To fix this, click on the "Content: Title" link in the "Fields" section. Tick the "Create a label" checkbox. Enter **Event** in the "Label" field. Click the "Apply (all displays)" button.

11. To make a more useful interface, we can take advantage of some of the geographic information that is associated with these events. A list of countries will be added to the page, which people can use to find events just in a particular country. From the "Filter criteria" section click the "add" button. From the list of available filters select "Content: Event location (field_event_location:country)" and click the "Add and configure filter criteria" button. Tick the "Expose this filter to visitors, to allow them to change it" checkbox. Change the "Label" field to **Event country**. Leave the "Operator" settings with the default values. Click the "Apply (all displays)" button.

12. The events now need to be sorted by their date. From the "Sort criteria" section click the "add" button. Select "Content: Event date (field_event_date)" from the list of available sort criteria and click the "Add and configure sort criteria" button. Leave "Sort ascending" selected. Click the "Apply (all displays)" button.

13. The user might select a country such as Antarctica that has no events, so we could provide some text for when this happens. The "Advanced" section of the view configuration form has a "No results behavior" section. Here, click the "add" button. Select "Global: Text area" from the available behaviors. Click the "Add and configure" button. In the main text field, enter some text like **There are no events listed in that country**. Click the "Apply (all displays)" button.

14. Click the "Save" button on the top right to create the view. It should look something like Figure 4-14.

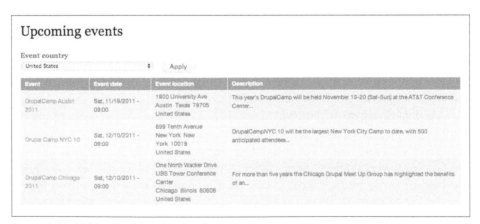

Figure 4-14. Table view of geographic data

The example above is a fairly simple one, and there are many other things that can be done with Views. A list or table view can be attached to a map view using a Views *attachment*, so that users can see a list of locations below the map.

Proximity is a useful piece of data to have. If you are using the Location module, its Views integration includes a proximity field (how close is this place to another place), a proximity *filter* (show me only things that are within 10 miles of this place), a proximity *argument* (like a proximity filter that can have the location changed through code), and *sort handlers* (do you want to see the nearest or furthest places first). There is also support for calculating the proximity to post codes, although this is only supported for a few countries and requires post code data to be loaded into your database. This process is outlined in the *INSTALL.txt* file of the module and on the Location handbook page (*http://drupal.org/documentation/modules/location*).

There is work in progress on an OpenLayers Proximity module (*https://github.com/jpstrikesback/proximity*) for Drupal 7. This will provide an *Exposed Filter* that will allow a user to enter their location and see a list of nearby content with distances.

Creating Feeds

In "Creating an OpenLayers Map Layer from KML" on page 59, a KML file was taken from an external source and displayed on a map. With Drupal it is easy to create a KML file like this for other sites to use. The KML module integrates with both the Location and Geofield modules; it just requires a latitude and longitude field. This example will extend the View created in "Spatial Data in Tables and Lists" on page 65 to create a KML file that includes Drupal events that people have added to the website, such as meetups, happy hours, and conferences.

1. Download and install the latest stable release of the KML module (*http://drupal .org/project/kml*). There is no permissions change or other configuration needed for this module.

2. Edit the Upcoming events view at *admin/structure/views/view/upcoming_events/ edit*.

3. At the top of the page click the "+ Add" button and add a "Feed."

4. The fields in this Feed Display will be different from the fields in the Page Display that we created before. The Title field will no longer be a link, because we do not have any particular need to bring people to our event details page. More importantly we need to include the latitude and longitude fields in this Display. Be sure to override the fields, otherwise the Page Display (the table we created earlier) will be changed, too.

   In the Fields section, edit the Title field. At the top of that screen, change the "For" drop-down from "All displays" to "This feed (override)." In the "Rewrite results" section, untick the "Output this field as a link" checkbox.

5. Add a new field, "Content: Event geo." In the configuration for this field, add a label of **Longitude**. In the "Formatter" drop-down, change to "Longitude only." Leave the "Format" as "Decimal degrees."

6. Repeat the previous step, setting the label and formatter to Latitude.

7. On the Feed details page, change the Format from "RSS Feed" to "KML Feed."

8. On the "Feed: Style options" screen, the "Field Usage" section is where the XML elements for the KML file are matched with fields in the Drupal View. Set the Name to "Content: Title," the Description to "Description," the Longitude to "Longitude," and the Latitude to "Latitude." Change the Filename to **drupal-events**. Click the "Apply" button to save.

9. In the Feed settings section, update the path to **drupal-events.kml**.

10. All of the other view settings will be inherited by the KML feed from the Page display, and can be left unchanged. Save the changes to the View.

11. You can now download the KML file at */drupal-events.kml* (or the path you set for the feed). The KML file can be viewed in Google Earth (*http://earth.google.com*) or uploaded to many different mapping services.

The Views module has caching that can be configured in the Advanced section of the Views interface. One fast and efficient way to display maps in Drupal is to create a KML file in Views, which is automatically cached; pulling that KML file into a map in OpenLayers is outlined in "Creating an OpenLayers Map Layer from KML" on page 59.

CHAPTER 5

Extending Map Interactions

The basics of mapping in Drupal are fairly simple: create your configuration in Drupal with PHP; send that configuration to the web browser; do a bit of custom JavaScript processing; and then let your chosen JavaScript library, such as Google Maps, do its magic. How this gets constructed varies from module to module; in the last two chapters we have shown how to build the basic setup with both Location and GMap, and with Geofield and OpenLayers. This chapter will focus on creating richer interactions for your users by adding onto those two architectures. With this understanding, you can do things like animate your map or display a real-time map of Foursquare checkins.

This will involve writing code. We do not expect you to be a Drupal rockstar, but we do make some basic assumptions: you know how to create a simple Drupal module, and you know what a Drupal hook is. The most advanced expectation is that you know the basics of how JavaScript is used in Drupal.

 If you have never written a Drupal module, don't worry, there is help to get you started. Read the Drupal.org documentation on how to write a module (*http://drupal.org/node/361112*). If you are unfamiliar with the Drupal API, there is a complete reference at api.drupal.org (*http://api .drupal.org/*). There is no definitive guide to JavaScript in Drupal, but a good place to start is the JavaScript section of Working with the Drupal API (*http://drupal.org/node/751744*).

In this chapter, we will go through an example of extending both the GMap module and OpenLayers module with HTML5 Geolocation functionality: the website user's position is imported from their smartphone or computer and the map is centered on them. Creating the same feature in both GMap and OpenLayers gives an insight into the differences in their architecture. If you are not familiar with HTML5 Geolocation, check out the W3C specification (*http://www.w3.org/TR/geolocation-API/*) or take a look at the geolocation demo from HTML5 Demos (*http://html5demos.com/geo*).

GMap

In previous chapters, the GMap module was used to improve the user interface for adding addresses to content ("Extending the Location module with the GMap module" on page 37) and also to integrate with Views to create maps of content ("Mapping with the GMap Module" on page 60). We will now dig into the module's architecture and use PHP and JavaScript to add the HTML5 Geolocation Behavior.

Architecture

The GMap module follows the standard method of mapping in Drupal: create a configuration object in the Drupal interface, then send the configuration object over to the web browser for the Google Maps JavaScript library to handle.

GMap stores its configurations as either a PHP *array* or a *macro* (see "Extending the Location module with the GMap module" on page 37 for an explanation of macros).

 The GMap module builds maps based on the default map defined at *admin/config/services/gmap*. This means that new map configurations that you create are overriding or adding to this default.

This GMap macro shows a satellite hybrid map centered on San Francisco:

```
[gmap zoom=9 |center=37.77071473849608,-122.24761962890625 |width=100%
 |height=300px |control=Small |type=Hybrid]
```

The macro above is equivalent to the following PHP array:

```
$map = array(
  'zoom' => '9',
  'width' => '100%',
  'height' => '300px',
  'maptype' => 'Hybrid',
  'controltype' => 'Small',
  'longitude' => '-122.24761962890625',
  'latitude' => '37.77071473849608',
  'id' => 'auto1map',
);
```

Each of these will generate a map that looks like look the one shown in Figure 5-1.

Geolocation Example

For our example, we will build a Drupal module that provides a geolocation Behavior for GMap by writing code that will hook into the GMap architecture. This module will work in two ways. First, there will be a link next to the map, which someone using the site can click to center the map on their location. Second, the administrator of the site

Figure 5-1. GMap macro example

will be able to change a setting so that whenever someone visits the website, the map automatically centers on their location. However, this will require each user to allow their phone or computer to access their location. The code for all of this will be done in a custom module called *mappingdrupal_gmap_extensions*. The steps for creating this module are:

1. Create a Drupal *block* to hold the link that can be used to update the map.
2. Hook into the GMap execution to add some options for the map.
3. Hook into the GMap execution to add some JavaScript.
4. Bind the geolocation interaction to the map with JavaScript.

This will create the interface shown in Figure 5-2.

Figure 5-2. GMap geolocation example

Creating the geolocation block

The block that we are creating will contain a link so that a user can allow our website to use their location to center the map on them. There is nothing specific to making maps in this first section; we are just creating a block.

The assumption here is that you have your *mappingdrupal_gmap_extensions.info* file defined and now are working in a blank *mappingdrupal_gmap_extensions.module* file.

The first step is to define our new block with hook_block_info() (*http://api.drupal .org/api/drupal/modules--block--block.api.php/function/hook_block_info/7*):

```php
<?php
/**
 * @file
 * Main module file for Mapping with Drupal GMap Extensions module.
 *
 * Provides basic examples to show how to extend the GMap module.
 */

/**
 * Implements hook_block_info().
 */
function mappingdrupal_gmap_extensions_block_info() {
  // Provide a block for user to choose to geolocate
  // themselves.
  $blocks['gmap_geolocate'] = array(
    'info' => t('GMap Geolocate'),
  );

  return $blocks;
}
```

The next step is to use the hook_block_view() (*http://api.drupal.org/api/drupal/ modules--block--block.api.php/function/hook_block_view/7*) function to create the link that will be displayed by the block:

```php
/**
 * Implements hook_block_view().
 */
function mappingdrupal_gmap_extensions_block_view($delta = '') {
  $block = array();

  switch ($delta) {
    case 'gmap_geolocate':
      $block['subject'] = t('Geolocate Yourself');
      $block['content'] = array(
        '#theme' => 'mappingdrupal_gmap_extensions_block_content',
      );
      break;
  }

  return $block;
}
```

For the block output, we are using Drupal Render Arrays (*http://drupal.org/node/930760*), a standard way of building a page in Drupal. We have to define a theme function for the rendering:

```
/**
 * Implements hook_theme().
 */
function mappingdrupal_gmap_extensions_theme($existing, $type, $theme, $path) {
  return array(
    'mappingdrupal_gmap_extensions_block_content' => array(
      'variables' => array(),
    ),
  );
}
```

Finally, we define the default implementation of the theme function. Our goal here is to create a link in HTML that we can reference from our JavaScript; we will do this with a specific class name, "mappingdrupal-gmap-geolocate-action." We will also hide this link using inline CSS in case the browser does not support HTML5 geolocation:

```
/**
 * Theme callback for block content.
 */
function theme_mappingdrupal_gmap_extensions_block_content() {
  return '<a class="mappingdrupal-gmap-geolocate-action"
    style="display:none;"></a>';
}
```

Add geolocation options to maps

Our next step is to add some configuration options to the "Map Behavior Flags" form at *admin/config/services/gmap*. These configuration options will allow the administrator of the site to decide whether users should be geolocated automatically, or whether the link to geolocate will be displayed. This is accomplished by using the hook_gmap() function provided by the GMap module.

 At the time of this writing, this functionality did not work as intended. The options are available in the configuration form, but the chosen settings were not available to our code when rendering the map. Later in this exercise, where the bug impacts our code, we provide a way to work around this problem. This issue should be resolved soon. For updates you can read the bug report in the GMap module's issue queue (*http://drupal.org/node/1339838*).

```
/**
 * Implements hook_gmap().
 */
function mappingdrupal_gmap_extensions_gmap($op, &$map) {
  // For documentation on this hook, look at the
  // gmap.php file in the gmap module.
```

```
switch ($op) {
  case 'behaviors':
    return array(
      'geolocate_auto' => array(
        'title' => t('Geolocate user automatically'),
        'default' => FALSE,
        'help' => t('This will geolocate the user on each page load and
          focus the map there.'),
      ),
      'geolocate_block' => array(
        'title' => t('Geolocate user with block link'),
        'default' => FALSE,
        'help' => t('This will geolocate the user only if they use
          the action on the GMap Geolocate block.'),
      ),
    );
}
}
```

The hook_gmap() function accepts an $op (operation) *parameter* to determine what part of rendering we are at, as well as a $map parameter so that we can alter the map along the way. The above code hooks into the behaviors operation to add two options: "Geolocate user automatically" and "Geolocate user with block link." You will see these options in the GMap interface at *admin/config/services/gmap* (Figure 5-3 shows the options).

Figure 5-3. GMap geolocation behavior options

There is some documentation on this hook found directly in the GMap module in the file *gmap.php*.

Add JavaScript

Now that we have the configuration, we need to add our client-side JavaScript (the code that runs in the user's browser to generate the map and our geolocation Behavior). We could add the JavaScript to every page though our module's `.info` file, but this would slow down the rest of the site by adding unnecessary JavaScript. We only need this JavaScript when maps are generated with the GMap module. Luckily, `hook_gmap()` gives us an opportunity to do things when the map is rendered and before the markup is generated, through the `pre_theme_map` operation. Let's add that now. The following is the `hook_gmap()` implementation. We use `drupal_add_js()` (*http://api.dru pal.org/api/drupal/includes--common.inc/function/drupal_add_js/7*) to include our Java-Script file:

```php
/**
 * Implements hook_gmap().
 */
function mappingdrupal_gmap_extensions_gmap($op, &$map) {
  // For documentation on this hook, look at the
  // gmap.php file in the gmap module.

  switch ($op) {
    case 'pre_theme_map':
      // We should check if the behavior is enabled, but it does not
      // seem to be available here.
      drupal_add_js(drupal_get_path('module', 'mappingdrupal_gmap_extensions') .
        '/mappingdrupal_gmap_extensions.js');
      break;

    case 'behaviors':
      return array(
        'geolocate_auto' => array(
          'title' => t('Geolocate user automatically'),
          'default' => FALSE,
          'help' => t('This will geolocate the user on each page load and
            focus the map there.'),
        ),
        'geolocate_block' => array(
          'title' => t('Geolocate user with block link'),
          'default' => FALSE,
          'help' => t('This will geolocate the user only if they use
            the action on the GMap Geolocate block.'),
        ),
      );
      break;
  }
}
```

Bind interactions to the map

Finally, we will bind some interactions to the map. Up until this point we were just setting things up; this is where we will actually make the map do something. The first step is to provide a basic container for the functionality and make a geolocation function to get the user's location from their phone or computer.

 We are using Drupal's *JavaScript Behaviors*. Behaviors in Drupal are a way of attaching JavaScript functionality to elements on a page. Almost all JavaScript written for Drupal should use Behaviors. Documentation on JavaScript for Drupal is a little sparse, but a good place is Managing JavaScript in Drupal (*http://drupal.org/node/756722*).

For finding the user's location, we use the HTML5 Geolocation API (*http://dev.w3.org/geo/api/spec-source.html*). Note that not all browsers can take advantage of this. It is supported by Internet Explorer 9 and later, Firefox 3.5 and later, Chrome 5.0 and later, Safari 5.0 and later, and Opera 10.60 and later.

```
/**
 * @file
 * Main JavaScript file for Mapping with Drupal GMap Extensions module.
 *
 * Provides geolocation functionality for a GMap.
 */

// Namespace $ for jQuery.  This ensures that $ will
// actually equal the jQuery function.
(function($) {

/**
 * Wrap handlers in a Drupal behavior so that
 * we can be sure that everything is available.
 */
Drupal.behaviors.mappingdrupal_gmap_extensions = {
  'attach': function(context, settings) {
    // The following ensures that the behavior is only performed
    // once.  Since we are adding a handler for all GMap maps,
    // we are not concerned with context.
    $('body').once(function() {

      // More code to go here later in the tutorial.

    });
  },

  // General function to geolocate user.
  'geolocate': function(map) {
    // First ensure that the HTML5 geolocation controls
    // are available.  We might use some more helpful
    // libraries for this, like Modernizr
    if (typeof navigator != 'undefined' &&
```

```
        typeof navigator.geolocation != 'undefined') {
        navigator.geolocation.getCurrentPosition(function (position) {
          lat = position.coords.latitude;
          lng = position.coords.longitude;
          map.setCenter(new google.maps.LatLng(lat, lng));
          map.setZoom(11);
        });
      }
    }
  };

  })(jQuery);
```

Let's break this down a bit. First, we wrap all our code in the following block to ensure that the dollar sign variable, $, is actually the jQuery function. This is important if there are other libraries included that want to use this variable:

```
// Namespace $ for jQuery.  This ensures that $ will
// actually equal the jQuery function.
(function($) {

// ...

})(jQuery);
```

The next part is where we use Drupal's Behaviors. The property that we add onto Drupal.behaviors is up to us, but it must be uniquely named, so it is good to prefix it with the name of your module:

```
/**
 * Wrap handlers in a Drupal behavior so that
 * we can be sure that everything is available.
 */
Drupal.behaviors.mappingdrupal_gmap_extensions = {

  // ...

};
```

Drupal Behaviors expect an attach function (and optionally a detach function) that will be fired whenever the Drupal.attachBehaviors method is called (for instance, on page load or when new elements are added with an AJAX call). Since we do not know how often Drupal.attachBehaviors will be called and why, we use the .once() method to ensure our code is only run once per page. We are adding this as a placeholder for now; we will add code to this part of the function in a later step of this tutorial:

```
    'attach': function(context, settings) {
      // The following ensures that the behavior is only performed
      // once.  Since we are adding a handler for all Gmap maps,
      // we are not concerned with context.
      $('body').once(function() {

        // More code to go here later in the tutorial.
```

```
    });
  },
```

Now we add our own custom method to `Drupal.behaviors.mappingdrupal_gmap_exten` `sions` to do the geolocation. Our method takes in the Google Maps API map object, then performs the HTML5 geolocation lookup; if a location is found, the map gets centered on it.

 This `geolocate` function could be in a separate JavaScript object, but since we already have this object to add to, this will help keep our code tidy.

```
// General function to geolocate user.
'geolocate': function(map) {
  // First ensure that that the HTML5 geolocation controls
  // are available.  We might use some more helpful
  // libraries for this, like Modernizr.
  if (typeof navigator != 'undefined' &&
    typeof navigator.geolocation != 'undefined') {
    navigator.geolocation.getCurrentPosition(function (position) {
      lat = position.coords.latitude;
      lng = position.coords.longitude;
      map.setCenter(new google.maps.LatLng(lat, lng));
      map.setZoom(11);
    });
  }
}
```

So far we have created a JavaScript behavior that will get a user's location. Now we need to write some code that will use the GMap module's JavaScript API to allow our geolocation behavior to change the map. Here is the complete JavaScript file:

```
/**
 * @file
 * Main JavaScript file for Mapping with Drupal GMap Extensions module.
 *
 * Provides geolocation functionality for a Gmap.
 */

// Namespace $ for jQuery.  This ensures that $ will
// actually equal the jQuery function.
(function($) {

/**
 * Wrap handlers in a Drupal behavior so that
 * we can be sure that everything is available.
 */
Drupal.behaviors.mappingdrupal_gmap_extensions = {
  'attach': function(context, settings) {
    // The following ensures that the behavior is only performed
    // once.  Since we are adding a handler for all GMap maps,
    // we are not concerned with context.
```

```
$('body').once(function() {
  // Add a handler to the map
  Drupal.gmap.addHandler('gmap', function(elem) {
    var gmap = this;

    // gmap (this) is the main gmap module with the following
    // main properties:
    // - map: The Google Maps API object.
    // - vars: The configuration passed from Drupal.
    //
    // elem is the DOM object that holds the Google Map.

    // The ready event is fired when things are ready with
    // the map.
    gmap.bind('ready', function() {
      // Normally should check the map object to see if the
      // geolocation behavior has been enabled for this website,
      // but it does not seem to be available.
      Drupal.behaviors.mappingdrupal_gmap_extensions.geolocate(gmap.map);

      // Again, we would normally check the map object to see
      // if this behavior has been enabled, but for some reason
      // this setting it is not available.
      //
      // We utilize jQuery to turn out block into a link
      // to update the map with user's location.
      $('.mappingdrupal-gmap-geolocate-action')
        .show()
        .html(Drupal.t('Find me on the map.'))
        .click(function(e) {
          Drupal.behaviors.mappingdrupal_gmap_extensions.geolocate(gmap.map);
          e.preventDefault();
        });
    });
  });
},

// General function to geolocate user.
'geolocate': function(map) {
  // First ensure that that the HTML5 geolocation controls
  // are available.  We might use some more helpful
  // libraries for this, like Modernizr
  if (typeof navigator != 'undefined' &&
    typeof navigator.geolocation != 'undefined') {
    navigator.geolocation.getCurrentPosition(function (position) {
      lat = position.coords.latitude;
      lng = position.coords.longitude;
      map.setCenter(new google.maps.LatLng(lat, lng));
      map.setZoom(11);
    });
  }
}
};
```

```
})(jQuery);
```

To interact with the map, we use the `Drupal.gmap.addHandler` JavaScript method, which allows us to interact with two things: the map object itself and the configuration that is specific to the GMap module:

```
Drupal.gmap.addHandler('gmap', function(elem) {
  var gmap = this;

  // gmap (this) is the main gmap module with the following
  // main properties:
  // - map: The Google Maps API object.
  // - vars: The configuration passed from Drupal.
  //
  // elem is the DOM object that holds the Google Map.

  // The ready event is fired when things are ready with
  // the map.

  // ....

)};
```

In this section of the JavaScript, since we have access to the map object, we can bind event handlers to the map object. Specifically, we will bind an event handler to the **ready** state, which is the event that happens when the map is first loaded by the user. Within this event handler, we do two things. The first is to geolocate the user as soon as the map is ready using our geolocation method we created above. The second is to display the link we created in our block which, when clicked, will do the same geolocation of the user:

```
// The ready event is fired when things are ready with
// the map.
gmap.bind('ready', function() {
  // Normally should check the map object to see if the
  // geolocation behavior has been enabled for this website,
  // but it does not seem to be available.
  Drupal.behaviors.mappingdrupal_gmap_extensions.geolocate(gmap.map);

  // Again, we would normally check the map object to see
  // if this behavior has been enabled, but for some reason
  // this setting it is not available.
  //
  // We utilize jQuery to turn out block into a link
  // to update the map with user's location.
  $('.mappingdrupal-gmap-geolocate-action')
    .show()
    .html(Drupal.t('Find me on the map.'))
    .click(function(e) {
      Drupal.behaviors.mappingdrupal_gmap_extensions.geolocate(gmap.map);
      e.preventDefault();
    });
});
```

And that is it! We now have a way of geolocating the user and centering the map to that location. In the next section, we will do the same task, but with the OpenLayers module.

OpenLayers

The OpenLayers module has been in development for a few years and has a more contemporary architecture and API than the GMap module. There is plenty of documentation around the OpenLayers module in the module's code and on Drupal.org (*http://drupal.org/*), but the easiest way to learn the API is to find something in the code that is similar to what you want to do and learn from that by adapting it.

Architecture

The OpenLayers module architecture is more complicated than the GMap module, but the basic structure is still the same as described at the beginning of this chapter: we create a configuration object in PHP; we send the object to the client (web browser) to be processed with JavaScript; and finally the object is rendered by the OpenLayers library. The main difference is that the OpenLayers module separates out aspects of the map creation into Layers, Styles, Behaviors, and Maps, as outlined in "Mapping with the OpenLayers Module" on page 47.

The architecture of the OpenLayers module is based on a widely used Drupal module called *CTools*. The CTools module (*http://drupal.org/project/ctools*) provides APIs and tools to do a broad range of things in Drupal more easily, including multistep forms, displaying modal windows, and handling AJAX requests. The most important role that the CTools module plays in OpenLayers is that it allows for *plug-ins*. CTools plug-ins is an architecture that activates code within other modules so that they carry out extra tasks or interact with one another in various useful ways. Layer Types and Behaviors are examples of CTools plug-ins. The Layer Types are plug-ins that handle the processing of different layers available for the map. Behavior plug-ins allow for interaction code to be added to the map (for instance the geolocation behavior, which is what we will do in this tutorial).

The other part of the CTools module that is used by OpenLayers is *exportables*. Layers, Styles, and Maps are all CTools exportables. A CTools exportable is a data record that can be stored in the database or exported in code. Exportables are covered in Chapter 7.

 The CTools module provides most of its documentation within the module itself, and this documentation will be available on your site if you enable the Advanced Help (*http://drupal.org/project/advanced _help*) module.

One straightforward example of an OpenLayers map configuration object is just the default map taken from the module itself. The map configuration object is an example of a CTools exportable. To see this exportable code, go to the OpenLayers maps page on your site at *admin/structure/openlayers/maps* and click the Export link next to one of the maps that you created in an earlier tutorial. Here is the code that you would export:

```
$default = new stdClass();
$default->api_version = 1;
$default->name = 'default';
$default->title = t('Default Map');
$default->description = t('This is the default map that comes
  with the OpenLayers module.');
$default->data = array(
  'projection' => '900913',
  'width' => 'auto',
  'height' => '400px',
  'default_layer' => 'osm_mapnik',
  'center' => array(
    'initial' => array(
      'centerpoint' => '0,0',
      'zoom' => '2'
    )
  ),
  'displayProjection' => '4326',
  'maxExtent' => openlayers_get_extent('4326'),
  'behaviors' => array(
    'openlayers_behavior_panzoombar' => array(),
    'openlayers_behavior_layerswitcher' => array(),
    'openlayers_behavior_attribution' => array(),
    'openlayers_behavior_keyboarddefaults' => array(),
    'openlayers_behavior_navigation' => array(),
  ),
  'layers' => array(
    'osm_mapnik' => 'osm_mapnik',
  )
);
```

This map is shown in Figure 5-4.

Figure 5-4. OpenLayers default map

Geolocation Example

We are going to build a Geolocation extension to the OpenLayers module, much like we did with the GMap example in "Geolocation Example" on page 70. This extension will do two things: first, it will geolocate the user and center the map on that position; second, it will provide a mechanism for the user to update the map with their position. Both of these will be configurable by administrators of the site.

OpenLayers already has a geolocation control that comes with the library itself, but only for the 2.11 version of the OpenLayers JavaScript library. The geolocation control that we will create will not depend on a specific version of the OpenLayers library. All the code for this example can be found in the custom module *mappingdrupal_ol_extensions*. The steps we will go through are the following:

1. Tell OpenLayers about our new Behavior.
2. Define the new Behavior plug-in object.
3. Geolocate the user with JavaScript.
4. Use CSS to clean up the appearance.

This will produce the map shown in Figure 5-5, although the map will show your own current location, rather than that of the author!

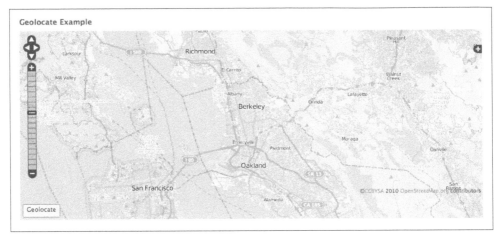

Figure 5-5. OpenLayers geolocation example

Define Behavior

OpenLayers Behaviors are defined and explained in "Exploring OpenLayers Behaviors" on page 57. Most of the Behaviors that come with the module are implementations of the OpenLayers library Controls (*http://docs.openlayers.org/library/controls.html*). The first step of our example is to tell OpenLayers about our new Behavior plug-in. This is done with hook_openlayers_behaviors(). The following is the complete .mod ule file (we are assuming you have already made your .info file):

```php
<?php
/**
 * @file
 * Main module file for Mapping with Drupal OpenLayers Extensions module.
 *
 * Provides basic examples to show how to extend the OpenLayers module.
 */

/**
 * Implements hook_openlayers_behaviors().
 */
function mappingdrupal_ol_extensions_openlayers_behaviors() {
  // For more documentation on writing OpenLayers behaviors,
  // see the docs/BEHAVIORS.txt within the OpenLayers module.

  return array(
    'mappingdrupal_ol_extensions_geolocate' => array(
      'title' => t('HTML Geolocate'),
      'description' => t('Allows for geolocation of the user
        utilizing HTML5.'),
      'behavior' => array(
        'path' => drupal_get_path('module', 'mappingdrupal_ol_extensions') .
          '/behaviors',
        'file' => 'mappingdrupal_ol_extensions_geolocate.inc',
        'class' => 'mappingdrupal_ol_extensions_geolocate',
```

```
        'parent' => 'openlayers_behavior',
      ),
    ),
  );
}
```

The `hook_openlayers_behaviors()` function returns an array, which has the ID of the Behavior as its key. This array contains another array with the following data:

- The `title` is the name of the Behavior and will show up in the administrative interface.
- The `description` is used in the administrative interface as well, to give guidance on the purpose of the Behavior.
- The `behavior` item is another array (Drupal loves nested arrays), describing where we will find the plug-in. This Behavior plug-in is a file.

The Behavior plug-in object

Now that we have told OpenLayers about where our Behavior plug-in file will be, we will need to create that file and define the Behavior behavior. We will add some configuration options to the Behavior so that the administrative user can choose how the map behaves. There are three options to be made available: whether to geolocate on page load; whether to create a button for geolocating; and what zoom level to go to when centering the map.

The first step is to create a subfolder in our module called `behaviors`. In that subfolder, we will create a new file named `mappingdrupal_ol_extensions_geolocate.inc`. The following is the complete file.

Our Behavior does not necessarily have to be in a `behaviors` folder. We defined the name of the file and where it lives in `hook_openlayers_behav iors()` in "Define Behavior" on page 84.

In upcoming versions of the OpenLayers module, Behaviors will be using a new CTools interface for plug-ins; this will involve telling CTools where plug-ins are found, and then putting the `.inc` files in this place along with some extra metadata. However, the method described here will still work.

```php
<?php
/**
 * @file
 * Implementation of OpenLayers behavior for HTML5 geolocation.
 */

/**
 * Geolocation behavior.
 */
class mappingdrupal_ol_extensions_geolocate extends openlayers_behavior {
```

```
/**
 * Provide initial values for options.
 */
function options_init() {
  return array(
    'on_load' => FALSE,
    'button' => TRUE,
    'zoom' => 11,
  );
}

/**
 * Provide form for configurations per map.
 */
function options_form($defaults) {
  return array(
    'on_load' => array(
      '#title' => t('Geolocate on load'),
      '#type' => 'checkbox',
      '#description' => t('When checked, the map will geolocate the user
        and zoom in when the map first loads.'),
      '#default_value' => isset($defaults['on_load']) ?
        $defaults['on_load'] : FALSE
    ),
    'button' => array(
      '#title' => t('Geolocate button'),
      '#type' => 'checkbox',
      '#description' => t('When checked, provides a button on the map that
        will geolocate the user.'),
      '#default_value' => isset($defaults['button']) ?
        $defaults['button'] : TRUE
    ),
    'zoom' => array(
      '#title' => t('Zoom level'),
      '#type' => 'textfield',
      '#description' => t('Determine the zoom level when geolocating.  Higher
        is more zoomed in.'),
      '#default_value' => isset($defaults['zoom']) ?
        $defaults['zoom'] : 11
    ),
  );
}

/**
 * Render.
 */
function render(&$map) {
  drupal_add_css(drupal_get_path('module', 'mappingdrupal_ol_extensions') .
    '/behaviors/mappingdrupal_ol_extensions_geolocate.css');
  drupal_add_js(drupal_get_path('module', 'mappingdrupal_ol_extensions') .
    '/behaviors/mappingdrupal_ol_extensions_geolocate.js');
  return $this->options;
}
```

That is a fair amount of code, but it is really only a few parts, so let's break it down:

```
/**
 * Geolocation behavior.
 */
class mappingdrupal_ol_extensions_geolocate extends openlayers_behavior {

  // ...

}
```

We define a new class. The class name mappingdrupal_ol_extensions_geolocate was defined in the first step of the example in "Define Behavior" on page 84, and it extends openlayers_behavior, which is a base class defined in the OpenLayers module. The mappingdrupal_ol_extensions_geolocate class contains several *methods*; the first of these methods is options_init():

```
/**
 * Provide initial values for options.
 */
function options_init() {
  return array(
    'on_load' => FALSE,
    'button' => TRUE,
    'zoom' => 11,
  );
}
```

The options_init() method returns an array of default values that we have now chosen for our configuration options:

```
/**
 * Provide form for configurations per map.
 */
function options_form($defaults) {
  return array(
    'on_load' => array(
      '#title' => t('Geolocate on load'),
      '#type' => 'checkbox',
      '#description' => t('When checked, the map will geolocate the user
        and zoom in when the map first loads.'),
      '#default_value' => isset($defaults['on_load']) ?
        $defaults['on_load'] : FALSE
    ),
    'button' => array(
      '#title' => t('Geolocate button'),
      '#type' => 'checkbox',
      '#description' => t('When checked, provides a button on the map that
        will geolocate the user.'),
      '#default_value' => isset($defaults['button']) ?
        $defaults['button'] : TRUE
    ),
    'zoom' => array(
      '#title' => t('Zoom level'),
      '#type' => 'textfield',
```

```
            '#description' => t('Determine the zoom level when geolocating.  Higher
              is more zoomed in.'),
            '#default_value' => isset($defaults['zoom']) ?
              $defaults['zoom'] : 11
        ),
    );
}
```

The options_form() method takes in default values from the map object, and returns
a Drupal form array for the configuration options of our Behavior. If you are unsure of
how to create this array, please see the reference on the Drupal Form API (*http://api
.drupal.org/api/drupal/developer--topics--forms_api_reference.html/7*). When adding or
editing maps, you can see these form items if you go to the OpenLayers Map interface
at *admin/structure/openlayers/maps*, and go to the Behaviors section. The form is shown
in Figure 5-6:

```
/**
 * Render.
 */
function render(&$map) {
  drupal_add_css(drupal_get_path('module', 'mappingdrupal_ol_extensions') .
    '/behaviors/mappingdrupal_ol_extensions_geolocate.css');
  drupal_add_js(drupal_get_path('module', 'mappingdrupal_ol_extensions') .
    '/behaviors/mappingdrupal_ol_extensions_geolocate.js');
  return $this->options;
}
```

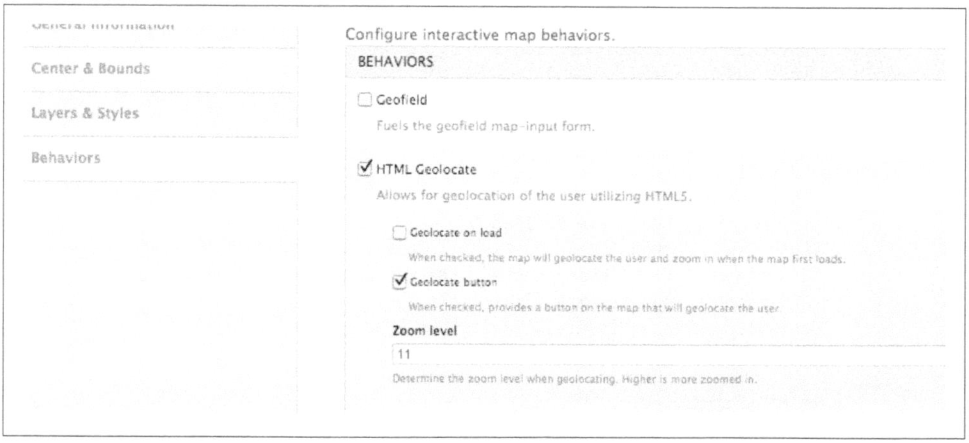

Figure 5-6. OpenLayers geolocation configuration

Finally the render() method is called when the map is rendered for display. The map
object is passed to the render() method in case there is any last-minute configuration
to add to the map. In our example, we are adding a JavaScript file to add interaction
to the map and a CSS file to make things look nicer.

JavaScript interactions

In the `behaviors` subfolder, create a new file named `mappingdrupal_ol_extensions_geo`
`locate.js`. As with the GMap module, we will be using Drupal Behaviors to interact
with elements on the page, including the OpenLayers map. First, set up the basic Drupal
Behavior and geolocation method:

```
/**
 * @file
 * JS Implementation of OpenLayers behavior for Geolocation.
 */

// Namespace $ to jQuery
(function($) {

/**
 * Geolocation Behavior
 */
Drupal.behaviors.mappingdrupal_ol_extensions_geolocate = {
  'attach': function(context, settings) {

    // ...

  },

  // Method to geolocate user.
  'geolocate': function(map, zoom) {
    // First ensure that the HTML5 geolocation controls
    // are available.  We might use some more helpful
    // libraries for this, like Modernizr
    //
    // We have to make sure we are explicit of the projection
    // as latitude and longitude are different from
    // spherical mercator (or other possiblilities).
    if (typeof navigator != 'undefined' &&
      typeof navigator.geolocation != 'undefined') {
      navigator.geolocation.getCurrentPosition(function (position) {
        var center = new OpenLayers.LonLat(
          position.coords.longitude,
          position.coords.latitude
        ).transform(
          new OpenLayers.Projection("EPSG:4326"),
          map.getProjectionObject()
        );
        map.setCenter(center, zoom);
      });
    }
  }
};

})(jQuery);
```

The first step is to define a new Drupal Behavior, `mappingdrupal_ol_extensions_geolo`
`cate`, and create an `attach` method for this Behavior. The `attach` method is empty at
this point; we will add code here later. The second step is to create a JavaScript

method for geolocating, `geolocate`, that accepts an OpenLayers map object and a zoom level.

Next we will add our OpenLayers Behavior wrapper within the `attach` method that we just created:

```
var data = $(context).data('openlayers');
if (data && data.map.behaviors['mappingdrupal_ol_extensions_geolocate']) {
  // Data about the map configuration and the map itself are stored
  // with jQuery's .data() functionality on the element that
  // contains the map.
  //
  // You can access the following from the data variable:
  // - data.map: The map configuration object.
  // - data.openlayers: The OpenLayers map object.

  // This makes it easy to reference the local behavior options.
  var options = data.map.behaviors['mappingdrupal_ol_extensions_geolocate'];

  // ...

}
```

The OpenLayers module uses the data() method of jQuery (*http://api.jquery.com/data/*) to store the map configuration settings. The settings are attached to the DOM element that contains our map. Our first step shown above is to get any data that is attached to the map object and check if OpenLayers data is stored there. We then check if our geolocation behavior is enabled. Finally, we add a an `options` variable that gets the configuration for our geolocation Behavior.

Next we will add the code that actually calls our `geolocate` method when necessary:

```
// First, check if the option to geolocate on load is
// enabled.
if (options.on_load) {
  Drupal.behaviors.mappingdrupal_ol_extensions_geolocate.geolocate(
    data.openlayers, options.zoom);
}

// Then check if a button was enabled.  We are utilizing
// OpenLayers Button and Panels Controls for this,
// but this could be any sort of button.
if (options.button) {
  var button = new OpenLayers.Control.Button({
    displayClass: 'mappingdrupal-ol-geolocate-button',
    title: Drupal.t('Geolocate'),
    trigger: function() {
      Drupal.behaviors.mappingdrupal_ol_extensions_geolocate.geolocate(
        data.openlayers, options.zoom);
    }
  });
  var panel = new OpenLayers.Control.Panel({
    displayClass: 'mappingdrupal-ol-geolocate-panel',
    defaultControl: button
  });
```

```
            panel.addControls([button]);
            data.openlayers.addControl(panel);
            panel.activate();
        }
```

We are doing two things here. First, we are checking the configuration of this map to see if the it should geolocate the user when they view it. If this setting is enabled, then the code calls our `geolocate` method.

Second, we are checking the configuration of this map to see if the geolocation button has been enabled. If so, we are adding this as an `OpenLayers Control Button`. The OpenLayers Control Button is a type of OpenLayers Control; you can see it defined in the OpenLayers documentation (*http://dev.openlayers.org/docs/files/OpenLayers/Control/Button-js.html*). As explained in that documentation, when the button is clicked, it calls the `trigger` function. In the code above, this trigger function is where we call our `geolocate` method.

Calling the `geolocate` method will update the center of the map based on the user's location and will zoom to the level that was chosen when configuring the map.

Here is the full JavaScript file for the example that we have just worked through:

```
/**
 * @file
 * JS Implementation of OpenLayers behavior for Geolocation.
 */

// Namespace $ to jQuery
(function($) {

/**
 * Geolocation Behavior
 */
Drupal.behaviors.mappingdrupal_ol_extensions_geolocate = {
  'attach': function(context, settings) {
    var data = $(context).data('openlayers');
    if (data && data.map.behaviors['mappingdrupal_ol_extensions_geolocate']) {
      // Data about the map configuration and the map itself are stored
      // with jQuery's .data() functionality on the element that
      // contains the map.
      //
      // You can access the following from the data variable:
      // - data.map: The map configuration object.
      // - data.openlayers: The OpenLayers map object.

      // This makes it easy to reference the local behavior options.
      var options = data.map.behaviors['mappingdrupal_ol_extensions_geolocate'];

      // First, check if the option to geolocate on load is
      // enabled.
      if (options.on_load) {
        Drupal.behaviors.mappingdrupal_ol_extensions_geolocate.geolocate(
          data.openlayers, options.zoom);
      }
```

```
        // Then check if a button was enabled.  We are utilizing
        // OpenLayers Button and Panels Controls for this,
        // but this could be any sort of button.
        if (options.button) {
          var button = new OpenLayers.Control.Button({
            displayClass: 'mappingdrupal-ol-geolocate-button',
            title: Drupal.t('Geolocate'),
            trigger: function() {
              Drupal.behaviors.mappingdrupal_ol_extensions_geolocate.geolocate(
                data.openlayers, options.zoom);
            }
          });
          var panel = new OpenLayers.Control.Panel({
            displayClass: 'mappingdrupal-ol-geolocate-panel',
            defaultControl: button
          });
          panel.addControls([button]);
          data.openlayers.addControl(panel);
          panel.activate();
        }
      }
    },

    // General function to geolocate user.
    'geolocate': function(map, zoom) {
      // First ensure that that the HTML5 geolocation controls
      // are available.  We might use some more helpful
      // libraries for this, like Modernizr
      //
      // We have to make sure we are explicit of the projection
      // as latitude and longitude are different from
      // spherical mercator (or other possiblilities).
      if (typeof navigator != 'undefined' &&
        typeof navigator.geolocation != 'undefined') {
        navigator.geolocation.getCurrentPosition(function (position) {
          var center = new OpenLayers.LonLat(
            position.coords.longitude,
            position.coords.latitude
          ).transform(
            new OpenLayers.Projection("EPSG:4326"),
            map.getProjectionObject()
          );
          map.setCenter(center, zoom);
        });
      }
    }
  };

})(jQuery);
```

The final touch

As you may have noticed, we included a CSS file in our Behavior plug-in. This is required to make our OpenLayers Control Button show up on the map. In the `behaviors` sub-directory, create a file named `mappingdrupal_ol_extensions_geolocate.css`:

```css
/**
 * @file
 * CSS for the Geolocation behavior
 */

.mappingdrupal-ol-geolocate-panel {
  bottom: 5px;
  left: 5px;
  z-index: 999999;
}

.mappingdrupal-ol-geolocate-buttonItemActive {
  background-color: #EEEEEE;
  border: 1px solid #666666;
  color: #222222;
  border-radius: 3px;
  height: 2em;
  width: 6em;
  text-align: center;
}

.mappingdrupal-ol-geolocate-buttonItemActive:after {
  content: "Geolocate";
}
```

 For the purpose of this tutorial, we used CSS to get the text "Geolocate" in our button. A better solution would be to use a background image in CSS.

The final button ends up on our map in the bottom left corner, as shown in Figure 5-7.

Figure 5-7. OpenLayers geolocation button

Putting all these steps together: you have created a custom module that extends the OpenLayers module to add geolocation and put your user in the middle of your map.

Conclusion

When working out how to add new ways of interacting with your maps, think about maps as configuration objects that can be processed by the appropriate module and library. The tutorials in this chapter have shown how these configuration objects are created, and have illustrated the different ways the architecture is handled by the GMap module and the OpenLayers module.

CHAPTER 6

Making Beautiful Maps

Over the last few years, thanks in a large part to Google Maps, people have become accustomed to using maps on the Internet. But because of the ubiquity of Google Maps, maps often have the feel of stock photography; they are very familiar and can be perceived as stale and impersonal. Recent developments in online mapping make it possible to use alternative map tiles and graphics, and even to create your own tiles.

This chapter covers various ways to make the look and feel of your map your own. We will show you how to customize markers, the map interface, map tiles, and map pop ups.

Markers

Even if you love the standard Google Map, you probably do not want to use the typical red pin to show the location of everything (see Figure 6-1). Fortunately, some other markers come with Drupal Modules, or alternatively you can add your own custom markers.

Figure 6-1. Google Maps typical marker

OpenLayers Styles

In "OpenLayers styles" on page 56 we showed how to add a new color of circular marker. As well as changing the line thickness, color, and opacity, it is possible to use images for markers. When adding a new style at *admin/structure/openlayers/styles*, you can enter the path to an image file in the "externalGraphic" field. Normally this file will be in your custom module or theme. Some examples of custom images used as markers are shown in Figure 6-2. An example of a vector used as a marker is shown in Figure 6-3.

Figure 6-2. OpenLayers styles marker example

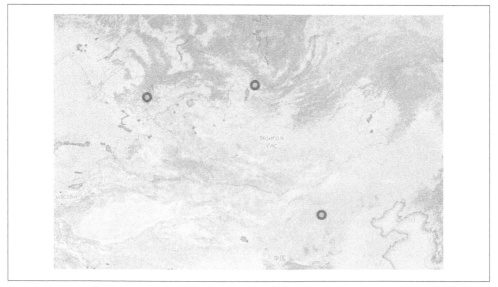

Figure 6-3. OpenLayers styles vector example

GMap Markers

The GMap module provides a number of default markers to use in your maps. But if these are not what you need, you will have to manually add new ones. The GMap module searches through the *markers* folder and all folders within that. It collects data on markers from *.ini* files and stores that data in a cached object. The module then references that object when creating and displaying maps. We will go through four steps to create a new marker:

1. Decide on a storage location for our markers and create a folder.
2. Add a Marker to that folder.
3. Create a *.ini* file and add details of our marker to the file.
4. Regenerate the marker cache.

 The GMap module provides documentation using the Advanced Help module (*http://drupal.org/project/advanced_help*). The page on your site that contains help for adding markers is *help/gmap/extending*.

Marker location

Unfortunately, GMap does not provide a good way to store our custom marker files. By default, all markers are stored in the GMap module within the `markers` directory. You can add your custom markers to this directory, but you will run into problems when you upgrade the module: you may forget that you put custom markers in this directory, and so will accidentally delete them.

The alternative is to change the variable that designates the directory that contains markers. However, because of the way that the GMap module works, only the markers that are available to use on our map are the markers in this directory. We could change this variable to a directory in our custom module, but then we would no longer have all the default markers that are included in the GMap module.

So, we lose in either case. For this example's purpose we will use the first method. We will create a new subdirectory in the GMap module called *mappingdrupal* and will end up with something like the following *<path_to_gmap_module>/markers/mappingdrupal/*.

Add a marker

Now, we will add the image file for our new marker to this directory. You can download the marker that we created for this exercise from MappingDrupal.com (*http://mapping drupal.com/sites/all/modules/contrib/gmap/markers/mappingdrupal/marker-black.png*). Save it as *<path_to_gmap_module>/markers/mappingdrupal/marker-black.png*. Make a note of the dimensions of the image (25×41), since we will need that later.

The .ini file

Next we need to tell GMap a little about our image so that it can put it into maps. Within our new directory, we create an .ini file (*http://en.wikipedia.org/wiki/INI_file*) named *mappingdrupal.ini* inside the subdirectory we created earlier (the name of the file is not important, but the .ini extension is). The file will be at *<path_to_gmap_module>/markers/mappingdrupal/mappingdrupal.ini*. This file can contain information about many markers, although in this example we just have one.

Add the following to that file:

```
; Defaults
[defaults]
;shadow = ""
anchorX = 15
anchorY = 41
infoX = 17
infoY = 6


; Marker sets
[mappingdrupal]
name = "Mapping Drupal Black"
sequence = "marker-black.png"
```

This defines a marker named *Mapping Drupal Black* shown on the map in Figure 6-4.

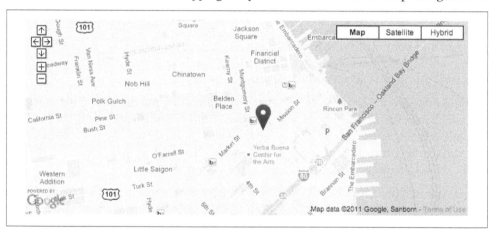

Figure 6-4. Displaying the Mapping Drupal marker in GMap

The following explains the different parts:

- The [defaults] section defines some default values for our marker. Defaults are useful when you have dozens of markers the same size. We have commented out the shadow line because this marker does not have a shadow. A shadow is a separate image file that is layered underneath the marker image.

- anchorX and anchorY define how the top left of the image should be offset so that the point of the pin is over the appropriate place on the map. In this case the point of the pin is the center of the bottom of the image, so anchorX should be half of the width of the image (15 pixels) and anchorY should be almost the full height of the image (41 pixels).

- infoX and infoY are the pixel coordinates relative to the top left of the marker image where the "tail" of a pop up points to. See "Theming Pop Ups" on page 104 for more on pop ups.

- [mappingdrupal] defines the marker set (see sequence below to see why it is a set) and is the identifier for the marker.

- name is the marker's text name, used to refer to it in the interface (see Figure 6-5).

- sequence defines the marker or markers that are used for this marker set. It is a sequence because we could use multiple images here, such as markers with numbers 1 through 9 on them.

Figure 6-5. Choosing the Mapping Drupal marker in GMap

Regenerate marker cache

Finally, we tell GMap to rebuild its marker cache. We can do this in the interface. Go to admin/config/services/gmap and under the *Regenerate Marker Cache* section, click on the button titled *Regenerate*. Then you can choose your new marker called *Mapping Drupal Black*, as shown in Figure 6-5. When shown on a map of San Francisco, it will look like Figure 6-4.

Data-Driven Styling

It is possible to change markers or styles based on data in your website. For example, a user can set the color of a marker, choosing a color when adding a new "Drupal User Group" to your website. This data-driven styling is achieved with *Marker Handling* in the GMap module, and with *Attribute Replacement* in OpenLayers. Both of these techniques are powered by the Views module, which includes the data needed for styling when doing the database query that creates the data layer for the map.

GMap Marker Handling

The GMap module uses Views to display Drupal data, as described earlier in "Mapping with the GMap Module" on page 60. The GMap Location module allows you to choose which markers to use based on Taxonomy Terms, Content Types, and User Roles. It is also possible to create a Field in your Content Type that contains a list of marker names. To select a marker for a particular content type, edit the content type and select a marker from the list. To use this setting when creating a map, you need to specify that in the "Marker handling" section of the View, as shown in Figure 6-6.

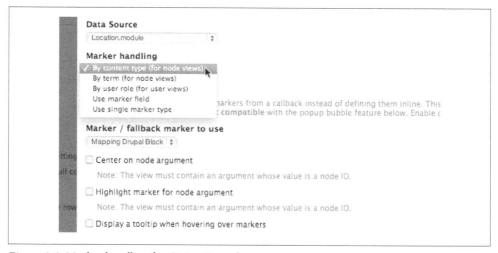

Figure 6-6. Marker handling for GMap Views formatter

OpenLayers Attribute Replacement

In the OpenLayers module, it is possible to replace any Style value with data, specifically Views data. To achieve this in the OpenLayers modules, we first have to tell Views that we want to use new some fields, then use a specific syntax to pass the data from the fields to our Style.

To do this, we will add a field to our Drupal User Groups content type from "Geofield Module" on page 29. This field will contain a list of colors. When a user is adding a new Drupal user group, they can choose a color from this list.

As shown in Figure 6-7, create a new field of type *Select (Text)* and add some colors to the "Allowed values list." Make this a required field; a missing color will cause errors when displaying the map.

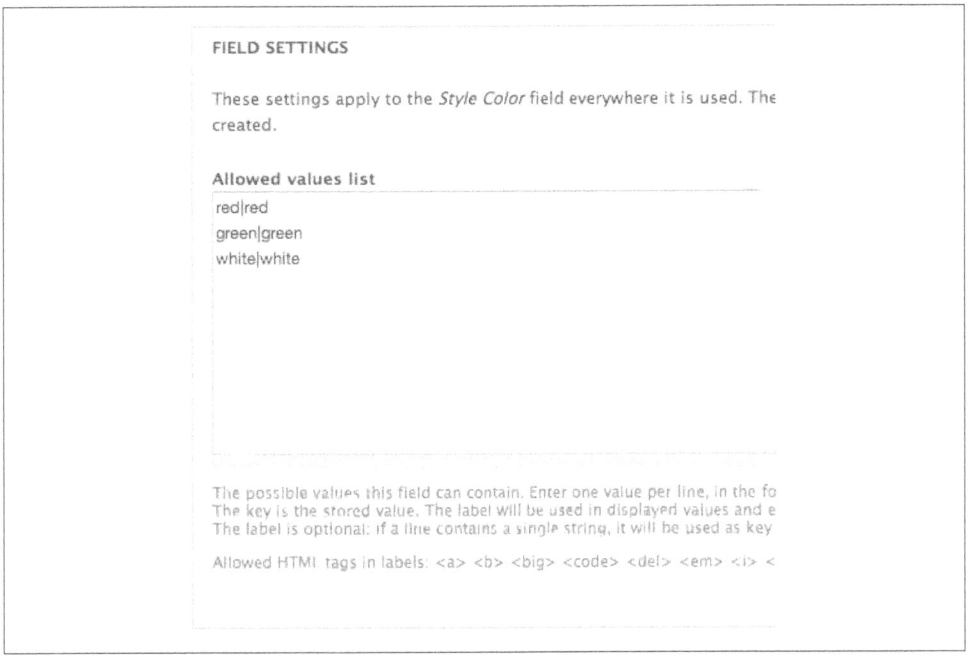

FIELD SETTINGS

These settings apply to the *Style Color* field everywhere it is used. The created.

Allowed values list

red|red
green|green
white|white

The possible values this field can contain. Enter one value per line, in the fo
The key is the stored value. The label will be used in displayed values and e
The label is optional: if a line contains a single string, it will be used as key

Allowed HTML tags in labels: `<a> <b> <big> <code> <del> <em> <i> <`

Figure 6-7. Values for Drupal Groups color field for OpenLayers Attribute Replacement

Next, add your new field to the View created earlier in "Setting Up an OpenLayers Map" on page 48. In the *Data Overlay View*, add your new field to the *Field List*. Now, if you look in the "Preview" section of the View, you will see a section that looks like Figure 6-8.

Copy **${field_style_color}** from this list of parameters, as this is the *Token* that will be replaced with the color for each Drupal user group that will be shown on the map.

The last step is to update our Style with this new Token value. Edit the Drupal User Groups style at *admin/structure/openlayers/styles/drupal_user_groups/edit* and change the fillColor field to the Token that you just copied, **${field_style_color}**. Edit the Drupal User Groups that have been added to your website to choose colors for them all. Your map should now have colored markers, as shown in Figure 6-9.

This has been a brief example, but enough to show how data associated with content on your website can be used to change styles used on your map.

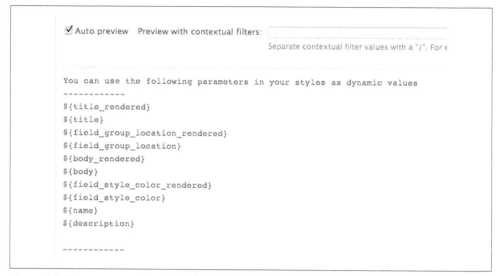

Figure 6-8. Views preview shows Attribute Replacement options

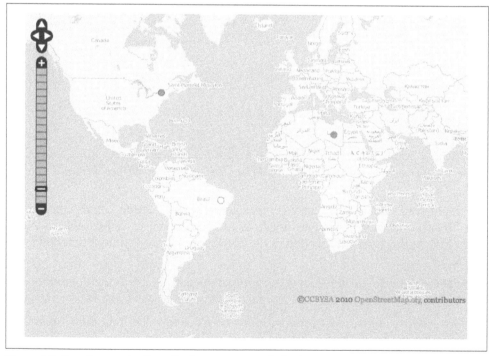

Figure 6-9. OpenLayers Attribute Replacement example final map

The Map Interface

Many different interface graphics are used when displaying a map: for instance, the zoom controls or the layer pickers. In the OpenLayers module, we can replace the default graphics with our own. This fairly simple change immediately makes your map more tightly integrated with your site.

OpenLayers Module

In OpenLayers, maps have two settings related to changing the interface graphics, the "Image Path" and the "CSS Location." The Image Path is the directory where Open-Layers will look for specifically named images to use in the interface. The CSS Location is the path to the CSS file that will be included with the map. Although you could include the CSS for styling your map in one of your Theme's CSS files, this is not a good idea, because lots of CSS is required for your map; you would end up loading lots of unnecessary CSS on pages that do not have maps.

 Both the Image Path and CSS Location are *Class level settings*, and will affect all subsequent maps on the page. This means that you will not be able to have two maps on the same page with different interface styles.

If you are using the default hosted version of the OpenLayers library, it will look in the following places for images and *.css* stylesheets:

- The default hosted directory of images: *http://openlayers.org/api/img/*
- The CSS located at: *http://openlayers.org/api/theme/default/style.css*

  The styles in this stylesheet often refer to images that are in a subdirectory at *http://openlayers.org/api/theme/default/img/*

 You can download the OpenLayers library directly from openlay-ers.org (*http://openlayers.org/*) and see all the images that are included.

These images and CSS create the default interface for OpenLayers, shown in Figure 6-10.

The best way to go about making your own image set is to start with the defaults from the OpenLayers library (*http://openlayers.org/*). Once you have downloaded and un-packed the library, you should copy the contents of the *<OpenLayers_library>/theme/default* directory into your Drupal installation (for instance, to *sites/all/libraries/mappingdrupal_ol_theme*). Next, to simplify things, copy all the images from *<OpenLayers_library>/img* into the directory *sites/all/libraries/mappingdrupal_ol_theme/img/*.

Figure 6-10. Default OpenLayers image set

Now replace images and edit the stylesheet. When you are done, in the OpenLayers map settings, enter the path to your images and CSS.

The map in Figure 6-11 shows the map interface that is soon to be the default for the OpenLayers module. It is a custom set compiled by community members.

Figure 6-11. Custom OpenLayers image set

Theming Pop Ups

Google Maps popularized the idea of a "pop up" on a map (Google calls this an *Info-Window*). A pop up is a speech bubble that appears when a user clicks on a marker; it displays a snippet of information relevant to that place, as shown in Figure 6-12.

Figure 6-12. Google Map traditional pop up

GMap Theming

In the GMap module, because of the way it uses Version Two of the Google Maps API, you cannot change what the pop up looks like. However, you do have control over the display of the content that goes into the pop up. GMap uses *Views Display* for rendering its output, so you can theme it just like any other View. Under the Advanced section in Views, you can see the Theme Information (shown in Figure 6-13). Create one of the *.tpl.php* files for the Row style output or Field content, such as *views-view-fields--drupal-companies--page.tpl.php*. Theming views is beyond the scope of this tutorial, but if you have the Advanced Help module (*http://drupal.org/project/advanced_help*) enabled, you can access the help page for theming views on your website at */help/views/using-theme*.

OpenLayers Theming

The simplest way to change the appearance of the pop up in OpenLayers is to use CSS. If you need to add or alter the markup, you will need to understand JavaScript theming.

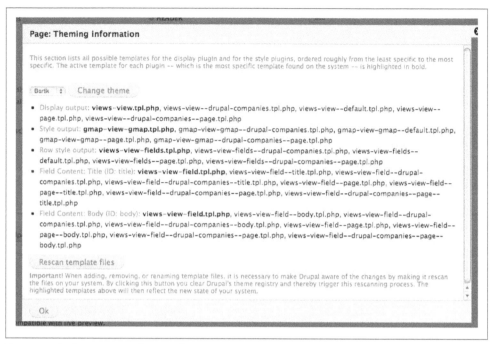

Figure 6-13. GMap Views theme information

The OpenLayers module uses Drupal's JavaScript Theming method. This is not as powerful as Views theming, because we are limited to using JavaScript rather than PHP, but we can achieve similar results. The following code is what the OpenLayers module uses to theme pop ups:

```
/**
 * Javascript Drupal Theming function for inside of Popups
 *
 * To override, define: Drupal.theme.openlayersPopup
 *
 * @param feature
 *  OpenLayers feature object.
 * @return
 *  Formatted HTML.
 */
Drupal.theme.prototype.openlayersPopup = function(feature) {
  var output = '';

  if (feature.attributes.name) {
    output += '<div class="openlayers-popup openlayers-tooltip-name">' +
      feature.attributes.name + '</div>';
  }

  if (feature.attributes.description) {
    output += '<div class="openlayers-popup openlayers-tooltip-description">' +
      feature.attributes.description + '</div>';
```

```
    }

    return output;
}
```

To override this theme, you need to define a `Drupal.theme.openlayersPopup()` method in a JavaScript file in your module or theme. The Drupal JavaScript API handbook page (*http://drupal.org/node/304258#js-theme*) explains how to do this (the documentation linked is for Drupal 6, but it will work for Drupal 7, too).

OpenLayers Pop Up Style

In "OpenLayers Module" on page 103, we saw how OpenLayers allows us to override images used in the map interface; the pop up can also be changed by following those instructions. The pop up is formed from a *CSS Sprite (http://www.alistapart.com/arti cles/sprites)* image that is named *cloud-popup-relative.png*. Figure 6-14 shows the image that gets used in the CSS Sprite; the thin outlines are hard to see, but it has several lines that make up edges, corners, and arrows that all get put together to form the pop up.

Figure 6-14. Original OpenLayers pop up sprite

Figure 6-15 shows a new image to replace to replace the default OpenLayers sprite image. The sprite creates a hard-corned translucent dark pop up. This pop up will soon be the default for the OpenLayers module.

Figure 6-16 shows how this pop up looks on a map.

Figure 6-15. Replaced OpenLayers pop up sprite

Figure 6-16. Replaced OpenLayers pop up final example

Map Tiles

Map tiles are small images tiled together to create a map, usually the base layer for a web map. A *tileset* is a specific set of these images. What tileset you choose can have a drastic effect on the visual nature of your map.

Adding Base Layers to GMap

GMap can be extended to add base layers. This has to be done directly with code. We will not go into great detail here, but will give a short overview.

1. To add some layer options in the GMap configuration form, we will use hook_gmap() again (this function was previously explained in "Add geolocation options to maps" on page 73). In hook_gmap(), for the baselayers operation, return an array structured like the following:

    ```
    $layers['Section Name']['layer_id'] = array(
      'title' => t('Title of layer'),
      'default' => TRUE,
      'help' => t('Description of layer'),
    );
    ```

2. Also, within hook_gmap(), in the pre_theme_map operation, use drupal_add_js() to include the JavaScript that will add the layer to the map.

3. Within the JavaScript file referenced in the previous step, include code similar to the following:

    ```
    Drupal.gmap.addHandler('gmap',function(elem) {
      var gmap = this;

      obj.bind('bootstrap_options', function() {
        var opts = gmap.opts;
        var layers = gmap.vars.baselayers;

        // Put layers here (??)
        opts.mapTypes.push();
        opts.mapTypeNames.push();
      });
    });
    ```

 The MapBox module (*http://drupal.org/project/mapbox*) has an implementation for adding base layers to GMap and will be the easiest way to do this, though it is still fairly undocumented. The MapBox module is discussed more at "MapBox" on page 112.

Adding Base Layers to OpenLayers

Adding base layers is one of the greatest strengths of the OpenLayers module. The module comes with support for Google Maps, OpenStreetMap, Bing, Yahoo!, Cloud-Made, and more. OpenLayers is intended as (and is) a versatile way of displaying almost any sort of geographical data.

Available Base Layers

Of the many base layers available, four will be discussed here: Google Maps, MapQuest, CloudMade, and MapBox, as well as a tool that lets you create your own map tiles.

Google Maps tiles

Both GMap and OpenLayers support the various Google Maps tilesets. These are fairly well known; they include a Road set, a Satellite set, a Hybrid of the two, and a Physical set that shows elevation and contour, shown in Figure 6-17.

Figure 6-17. Google Maps Physical layer

MapQuest tiles

MapQuest (*http://www.mapquest.com/*) was one of the original organizations doing web mapping. Recently they partnered with OpenStreetMap (*http://www.openstreet map.org/*), an online, open (wiki-style) map of the world. MapQuest has released a free tileset based on the OpenStreetMap data (shown in Figure 6-18), as well as a free tileset of satellite imagery (shown in Figure 6-19). You can find out more about these and the associated API in their developer documentation (*http://developer.mapquest.com/web/ products/open/map*).

In upcoming versions of the OpenLayers modules, these new layers will be available by default.

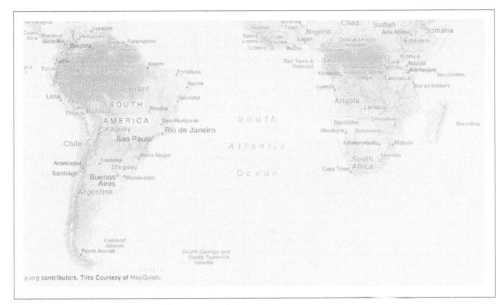

Figure 6-18. MapQuest's OpenStreetMap tiles

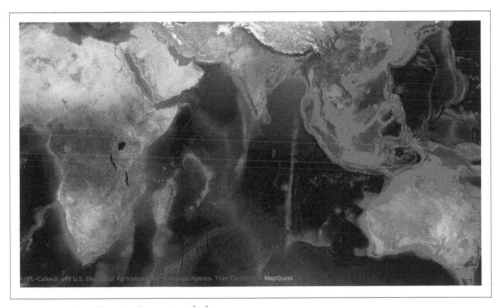

Figure 6-19. MapQuest's Open Aerial tiles

CloudMade

CloudMade (*http://cloudmade.com/*) provides location-based services. Their Style Editor (*http://developers.cloudmade.com/projects/show/style-editor*) is a free web-based tool for creating custom tilesets from OpenStreetMap data. This is the easiest and most inexpensive way to get custom map tiles for your site. Figure 6-20 is a screenshot from the Style Editor showing some of the styles that people have created.

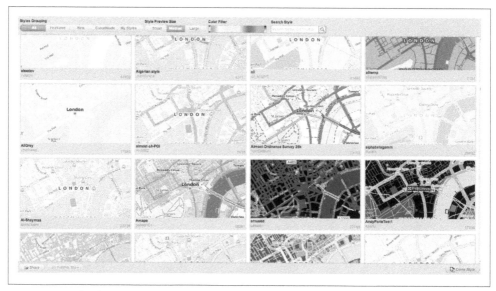

Figure 6-20. CloudMade Style Editor browser

The OpenLayers module has support for CloudMade tilesets. This requires downloading another library, but there are instructions within the module at *admin/structure/openlayers/layers/settings*.

MapBox

Development Seed (*http://developmentseed.org/*) is a company that has made a suite of open source mapping tools, known as MapBox (*http://mapbox.com*). Among their many great contributions to the open source world, a lot of their tilesets are available to use for free. You can browse them at tiles.mapbox.com (*http://tiles.mapbox.com/*).

There is a MapBox module (*http://drupal.org/project/mapbox*) that provides base layers to both GMap module and the OpenLayers module. With the OpenLayers module, you can add a wide selection of MapBox base layers from the many tilesets, while the GMap integration only provides a select few. The MapBox module also provides a number of nice icons for use in the OpenLayers module.

TileMill

TileMill (*http://mapbox.com/tilemill/*) is part of the MapBox suite of tools. TileMill makes it possible to create custom tilesets from your own data sources. It runs as an application on Mac OS X or Ubuntu, takes in multiple data sources, and uses a CSS-like style language called Carto to create tilesets that can then be exported for use in your maps. TileMill is a great way to make tilesets, but it does not include a way to host them to use in web applications. Serving tilesets is handled by another MapBox product called TileStream (*https://github.com/mapbox/tilestream*), or by configuring your own very fast map tile server.

CHAPTER 7

Managing Maps as Features

Throughout the tutorials in this book, all the configuration has been done through the user interface. Drupal stores this configuration in your database, which is a problem for two main reasons:

1. It is difficult to manage these changes when deploying or changing environments.
2. There is no history log of modifications.

One tool that has been developed over the last couple of years to solve this is the Features module (*http://drupal.org/project/features*). With the Features module, all the work you have done configuring your map settings can be bundled up and saved in a handy format. You can then reuse the configurations in your next mapping project, and share them with other Drupal developers. Your settings can be easily backed up with *version control*. For more background on Features, see the Features handbook page (*http://drupal.org/node/580026*).

Features is well supported by OpenLayers and Geofield. Much of the configuration for maps built with GMap and Location is based on Views, which also has good support for the Features module. In this section we will walk through the process of exporting your map configurations to Features.

 There are other ways to export configuration to code, such as CTools export, but the Features module is the simplest to use.

The first step is to set up the Features module and another module that helps with this process: the Strongarm module.

1. Download the latest stable release of the Features module (*http://drupal.org/project/features*) and the Strongarm module (*http://drupal.org/project/strongarm*) to your site's Modules directory.
2. Enable the Features module.

3. Configure the permissions for the Features module at *admin/people/permissions#module-features*. The administrator role should have permission for both "Administer features" and "Manage features."

Exporting OpenLayers and Geofield with Features

In this chapter, names of various Modules, Fields, Content Types, etc., may be different from what you have in your site, and some things won't be there if you did not complete all of the tutorials. This Feature will contain the configuration for the Content Types, Views, and Maps, Styles, etc., that we created to demonstrate OpenLayers and Geofield in earlier chapters. This was based around Drupal User Groups and Drupal Events.

1. From the Manage features page, create a new Feature at *admin/structure/features/create*.

2. In the "Name" field, enter **User groups and events**.

3. In the "Description" field, enter **Configuration for user groups and events**.

4. The "Version" and "URL of update XML" fields can be left blank, as they are only needed if you plan to distribute your Features beyond your own site.

5. The "Edit components" section of the form is the where you choose which of the available configurations you want to include in your Feature. It is easiest to start with the most important pieces of configuration. The Features module has a fairly sophisticated set of dependency-checking logic, so it will detect much of the other configuration for you.

6. In the "Edit components" drop-down, select "Content types: node." In the list of content types, select "Event" and "User Group." These are the two content types that were used in the tutorials for making maps with OpenLayers and Geofield. Notice how those two content types now show up in gray on the right and many other things in other sections will now suddenly show up in blue. These are the other parts of the configuration that Features will export to code without any further instruction on your part; this is the dependency checking.

7. In the "Edit components" drop-down, select "OpenLayers: openlayers_layers." There is nothing listed here to add to our Feature, because all the layers were created in Views, which Features handles separately.

8. In the "Edit components" drop-down, select "OpenLayers: openlayers_maps." In the list of maps, select "Drupal user groups." This is the Map that was configured in "OpenLayers Maps" on page 52.

9. In the "Edit components" drop-down, select "OpenLayers: openlayers_styles." In the list of styles, select "Drupal user groups." This is the style that was configured in "OpenLayers styles" on page 56.

10. In the "Edit components" drop-down, select "Permissions: user_permission." In the very long list of permissions, find any that relate to the modules that are part of this feature:

- Node: Event: Create new content
- Node: Event: Edit own content
- Node: Event: Edit any content
- Node: Event: Delete own content
- Node: Event: Delete any content
- Node: User Group: Create new content
- Node: User Group: Edit own content
- Node: User Group: Edit any content
- Node: User Group: Delete own content
- Node: User Group: Delete any content
- OpenLayers UI: Administer OpenLayers

11. In the "Edit components" drop-down, select "Strongarm: variable." In the very long list of variables, find any that relate to this feature:

- openlayers_default_map
- openlayers_source

12. In the "Edit components" drop-down, select "Views: views_view." In the list of Views, select "Drupal groups," "Map of Drupal groups," and "Upcoming events." These are the Views that were used to make the maps and other tutorials for OpenLayers and Geofield.

13. The Feature is now complete. At the bottom of the page, click the "Download feature" button. Extract the downloaded file to your site. This downloaded Feature is a special sort of module, and it is usually placed in a separate directory, such as in *sites/all/modules/features* or *sites/default/modules/features*, as shown in Figure 7-1.

14. The new Feature is disabled by default. At *admin/structure/features* on the Manage Features page, tick the checkbox next to the "User groups and events" Feature and click the "Save settings" button to enable the Feature.

All of the configuration for the Content Types, Views, and Maps for User Groups and Events are now stored in code. This code can be added to version control and moved between development and production sites. For more details on managing Features, see the Features handbook page (*http://drupal.org/node/580026*).

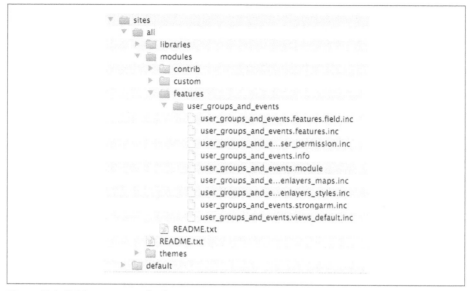

Figure 7-1. Folder structure for features

Exporting GMap and Location with Features

As in the previous tutorial, some of the names or configurations might be different from what is shown below, depending on which of the tutorials you completed throughout the book. This Feature will contain the configuration for the Content Types and Views that we created to demonstrate GMap and Location in earlier chapters. This was based around Drupal Companies.

1. From the Manage features page, create a new Feature at *admin/structure/features/ create*.

2. In the "Name" field, enter **Drupal companies**.

3. In the "Description" field, enter **Configuration for Drupal companies**.

4. In the "Edit components" drop-down, select "Content types: node". In the list of content types, select "Drupal Company."

5. In the "Edit components" drop-down, select "Permissions: user_permission." In the very long list of permissions, find any that relate to the modules that are part of this feature:

   • GMap Macro Builder: Create gmap macro
   • Location: Submit latitude/longitude
   • Node: Drupal Company: Create new content
   • Node: Drupal Company: Edit own content
   • Node: Drupal Company: Edit any content
   • Node: Drupal Company: Delete own content

- Node: Drupal Company: Delete any content

6. In the "Edit components" drop-down, select "Strongarm: variable." In the very long list of variables, find any that relate to this feature. This is rather difficult for the Location module, because it creates a variable for every country in the world. Try to find the ones that relate to the countries you care about, though only the two-letter country codes tell you which is which:

- gmap_default
- gmap_marker_file
- gmap_markermanager
- gmap_mm_type
- location_default_country
- location_defaultnum_drupal_company
- location_display_location
- location_general_geocoders_in_use
- location_geocode_google_minimum_accuracy
- location_geocode_google_apikey

 Be careful about exporting the Google Maps API key to code. It only works for domains with the same URL. So if you have a development site at exampletest.com and a production environment at example.com, you will need a different API key for each.

- location_geocode_au
- location_geocode_ca
- location_geocode_dk
- location_geocode_cs
- location_geocode_fr
- location_geocode_gb
- location_geocode_jp
- location_geocode_us

7. In the "Edit components" drop-down, select "Views: views_view." In the list of Views, select "Drupal companies." This is the View that was used to make the map for Location and GMap in Chapter 4.

8. The Feature is now complete. At the bottom of the page, click the "Download feature" button. Extract the downloaded file to your site and put it in the location where you put the Feature from the previous exercise.

9. The new Feature is disabled by default, so enable it on the Features page at *admin/structure/features*.

Exporting your map configuration to code may take a little time, but it will save time and effort in the long term. If you are new to web development, it is worth learning to use a version control system to manage your code. *Git* has become the main version control system used with Drupal. The Drupal documentation for Git (*http://drupal.org/documentation/git*) is useful, but if you are totally new to version control, the GitHub help (*http://help.github.com/*) is an easy introduction.

CHAPTER 8

Conclusion

With all that you have learned about mapping with Drupal, you should now be able to create beautiful and useful maps for your website. Even using the pre-existing Drupal modules, you can build appropriate, useful, and interactive maps. Going beyond that, you can create your own modules to add imaginative and lively ways for your site's users to interact with the maps, and you can personalize the maps with custom-built markers and interfaces.

Next Steps in Mapmaking

If you want to create even more interesting maps, with features that are not available through existing Drupal modules, you need to become familiar with JavaScript and with the JavaScript libraries that are used to create maps.

If you are using the OpenLayers module, get to know the OpenLayers JavaScript library. "OpenLayers" on page 81 explained how to add new JavaScript Behaviors to your maps. There are many Behaviors in the OpenLayers JavaScript library that are not implemented in the OpenLayers module, but which you can activate using the method in Chapter 5. For example, it would be possible to add a shape on your map that rotates, with the speed of rotation representing the intensity of a tornado. The OpenLayers examples page (*http://openlayers.org/dev/examples/*) contains an example showing the *geometry.rotate* method. Then again, you could create labels on your map that change depending on the zoom level. Find an example that is close to what you want to do, then view its source code to work out how it achieves its effect. In conjunction with that, study the class documentation (*http://dev.openlayers.org/releases/OpenLayers-2 .11/doc/apidocs/files/OpenLayers-js.html*). For the rotating tornado, you would read the documentation for the OpenLayers.Geometry.LineString class (*http://dev.openlayers .org/releases/OpenLayers-2.11/doc/apidocs/files/OpenLayers/Geometry/LinearRing-js .html#OpenLayers.Geometry.LinearRing.rotate*). There is one book in English on OpenLayers, which is listed in Appendix A.

As mentioned in "Mapping with the OpenLayers Module" on page 47, the OpenLayers JavaScript library is an open source project, so if you are running into limitations on what is possible and are inspired to add new features, you can get involved and contribute code (*http://trac.osgeo.org/openlayers/wiki/HowToContribute*). The OpenLayers email lists (*http://trac.osgeo.org/openlayers/wiki/MailingLists*) are the best way to stay current with new developments.

If you are using the GMap module, you will want to understand the Google Maps API (*http://code.google.com/apis/maps/index.html*). That API has several subsidiary APIs within it. The Web Services API is useful if you want to geocode an address, generate driving directions, or get the elevation of a point. The Maps Image APIs allow you to create an image of a map or *Street View* and display that on your website without using any JavaScript. Most relevant to the Drupal GMap module, however, is Version 2 of the Google Maps JavaScript API (*http://code.google.com/apis/maps/documentation/javascript/v2/*). This is the code that allows you to embed maps on your website using JavaScript, and this is how you can change the way that maps work and what is displayed on them. For example, if you wanted to change the zoom controls of your map from images to text, the instructions and example are in the documentation for map controls (*http://code.google.com/apis/maps/documentation/javascript/v2/controls.html #Custom_Controls*). If you wanted to make a map of the world that plays the national anthem of each country you click on, the JavaScript API Reference (*http://code.google .com/apis/maps/documentation/javascript/v2/reference.html*) is where you would look for the code to do this. In addition to that documentation, there is a code playground (*http://code.google.com/apis/ajax/playground/?exp=maps#directions_advanced*), where all of the examples are listed and you can view the source code, change that code on the page, and then see how your changes come out on the map. Several books have been written on Google Maps, some of which are listed in Appendix A.

The Future of Mapping with Drupal

There are exciting developments all the time in open source mapmaking, and there is work being done to integrate these into Drupal. The new ideas at the moment are in two main fields: displaying maps and data storage.

There are several new JavaScript libraries for displaying maps, including Leaflet (*http: //leaflet.cloudmade.com/*), which was introduced in "Library size" on page 23. The Leaflet project is to make maps display well on both mobile and desktop browsers, and to take advantage of HTML5 to be fast and have a small file size. The code is *object-oriented*, an architecture that is used to make the code modular and extensible. If you are interested in making open source maps that are fast and work well on mobile browsers, this is a project to work with.

The options for spatial data storage are improving, both in Drupal and in other open source projects. Some of the challenges and solutions were discussed in "Databases" on page 21. A couple of Drupal modules, PostGIS (*http://drupal.org/sandbox/geops/*

1212962) and GeoServer (*http://drupal.org/sandbox/geops/1314208*), are worth watching if you are working with especially vast databases and are attracted by the idea of integrating spatial databases into Drupal.

Another interesting development is integrating *Apache Solr* search for spatial data into Drupal. Solr (*http://lucene.apache.org/solr/*) is a fast open source search platform written in the Java programming language. It is much faster than searching using database queries, which is how search is done by default in Drupal. As well as geospatial search, Solr allows search results to be sortable and handles *faceted search* (navigating search results by multiple filters, such as showing only restaurants that serve brunch and are wheelchair-accessible). The Apache Solr module (*http://drupal.org/project/apachesolr*) integrates Solr with Drupal, but it does require you to run Java on your web server in addition to PHP. The OpenLayers Apache Solr module (*http://drupal.org/project/open layers_solr*) then integrates many of the modules mentioned earlier in this book (Geofield, Geocoder, and OpenLayers) with LocalSolr (*http://www.gissearch.com/local solr*). The OpenLayers Apache Solr module provides a map, layer, layer type, and block for OpenLayers.

There is an initiative within the Mapping and Location Group in Drupal to pull together all the disparate modules into a *Geo Content Management System*. The Geo module (*http://drupal.org/project/geo*) was an attempt to do this, and it has been widely and intensely discussed at DrupalCons (the twice-yearly Drupal conferences). The subject was raised in 2007 in Bdragon's vision for doing locations "right" in Drupal (*http://groups.drupal.org/node/6089*) and more recently in a post started by one of this book's authors, summarizing the Drupal geo stack (*http://groups.drupal.org/node/138884*). The goal of this broad initiative is to separate out all of the different parts of mapping in Drupal (data storage, data input, searching spatial data, geocoding, and displaying maps) so that developers can choose which module they want to use for each part.

There are many ways to get involved in making maps in Drupal, so jump into whatever interests you most. Drupal developers use *IRC* (Internet Relay Chat) both to get help and to discuss module development. There is an introduction to IRC on the Community and Support page (*http://drupal.org/irc*). Mapping is discussed in the *#drupal-geo* channel. The other way to keep up with new developments and initiatives is to join the Location and Mapping Group (*http://groups.drupal.org/location-and-mapping*) on *http://groups.drupal.org/*.

Over the next few years, the power of Drupal to make lively, useful interactive maps will only increase, the modules becoming more straightforward to use even as the options available become more flexible and creative. One thing's for sure, there is no longer any excuse for offering information about places and locations without presenting that information the proper way, on a map. And there's no longer any excuse for that map to be unhelpful, unresponsive, or boringly just like all the other maps. For inspiration we'll leave you with one of the most beautiful and engaging maps to be made with Drupal for Energy.gov, shown in Figure 8-1. Happy mapping!

Figure 8-1. Energy.gov contains many beautiful maps. This map shows how much energy, waste and money has been saved by energy audits. It was built by Treehouse Agency using Drupal 7, MapBox, Geofield, OpenLayers, Apache Solr, OpenLayers Apache Solr, and Geocoder.

Further Reading

There is a huge amount of documentation for Drupal on drupal.org (*http://drupal.org*); however, there are also some books that we recommend.

Drupal Books

Drupal has become a very popular platform over the past few years, and as a result, there are a number of Drupal books focused on many different subjects. The following are just a few of the books we know to be good, but there are many more; please check out the list of books on Drupal.org (*http://drupal.org/books*), or an Amazon search for Drupal books (*http://www.amazon.com/s/ref=nb_sb_noss?url=search-alias%3Dstrip books&field-keywords=drupal&x=0&y=0*).

Lynn Beighley and Seamus Bellamy, *Drupal For Dummies*. (Hoboken: For Dummies, 2011)

Matt Butcher, Larry Garfield, John Wilkins, Matt Farina, Ken Rickard, Greg Dunlap, *Drupal 7 Module Development*. (Birmingham: Packt, 2010)

Benjamin Melancon, Allie Micka, Amye Scavarda, Benjamin Doherty, Bojhan Somers, Jacine Rodriguez, Karoly Negyesi, Moshe Weitzman, Roy Scholten, Ryan Szrama, Sam Boyer, Stephane Corlosquet, Amanda Miller-Johnson, Andrew Grice, Dan Hakimzadeh, Kasey Dolin, Stefan Freudenberg, and Jacqueline Aponte, *The Definitive Guide to Drupal 7* (New York: Apress, 2011)

Mapping Theory Books

The following is a short list of books around the theory of mapping and cartography, specifically ones that challenge the traditional view of maps in our culture.

Mark Monmonier, *How to Lie with Maps*. (Chicago: The University of Chicago Press, 1996)

Denis Wood, *Rethinking the Power of Maps*. (New York: Guilford Press, 2010)

Denis Wood and John Fels, *Cartographic Constructions of the Natural World*. (Chicago: The University of Chicago Press, 2008)

Technical Mapping-Related Books

The following is a short list of books that are useful for different aspects of web mapping. Unfortunately there is not a great recent book that provides an overview of web mapping.

David Flanagan, *JavaScript: The Definitive Guide*. (Sebastopol, CA: O'Reilly, 2011)

Erik Hazzard, *OpenLayers 2.10*. (Birmingham: Packt, 2011)

Michael Purvis, Jeffrey Sambells, and Cameron Turner, *Beginning Google Maps Applications with PHP and Ajax*. (New York: Apress, 2006)

Gabriel Svennerberg, *Beginning Google Maps API 3*. (New York: Apress, 2010)

Map Projections

This appendix describes some common and uncommon map projections. Introduced in "Projections and Coordinate Systems" on page 11, map projections are the many different ways of translating the shape of the Earth, which is like sphere, onto a flat surface.

 For a much more in-depth look at the many different kinds of projections there are and what benefits and disadvantages they possess, with pictures, Map Thematics has an amazing list of projections (*http://www.mapthematics.com/ProjectionsList.php*).

WGS 84 (Latitude and Longitude)

The World Geodetic System (19)84 projection is a variant of the Mercator projection, but without the assumption that the Earth is a sphere (actually an ellipsoid). This is the projection that GPS systems use. It has the same limitations of the Spherical Mercator that were discussed in "Projections and Coordinate Systems" on page 11. When you get to the local level of detail on a map, you will find slight differences in position from the spherical Mercator.

 The WGS 84 projection has the EPSG:4316 identifier.

Gall-Peters Projection

The Gall-Peters projection represents the world in a rectangle, but preserves area. This is a stark difference from a Mercator projection, as it address the Greenland problem (in a Mercator projection, Africa and Greenland look the same size; Greenland is actually around one-tenth the area of Africa). You will not usually find this projection used in web mapping.

 The West Wing, an American TV show, has a fun episode where a side storyline involves this projection. The White House press secretary is presented with a Peters world map and is taken aback by the difference in the world view. The video clip and explanation are on the ODT Maps (*http://odtmaps.com/what_they_are_saying/west-wing.asp*) website.

South-Oriented Maps

A south-oriented map puts south at the top of the map and north at the bottom. This is an important (and shocking to some) notion, as the idea of "north on top" is an arbitrary designation. The ubiquity of north-oriented maps is believed to have a significant effect on our view of cultures in the north and south.

Though not a projection, a popular map that has this orientation is the McArthur's Universal Corrective Map of the World.

You will be very hard pressed to find a web map that is south-oriented, but there is work being done to make this a much easier task. As of recent, there is an official projection code for a Transverse Mercator (South Oriented): EPSG:9808.

Glossary

This appendix is a list of mapping and Drupal terms that may need further explanation. We link to further details when possible.

Mapping Terms

The following are mapping terms that are used throughout the book:

API

An *Application Programming Interface* (API) is code that is either by itself or part of a larger application that provides a way for other software to communicate with it. For instance, the Drupal API (*http://api.drupal.org/*) provides methods for modules to hook into the various parts of the Drupal system.

For more detail, see the Wikipedia article for API (*http://en.wikipedia.org/wiki/Application_programming_interface*).

GeoJSON

GeoJSON is another format for describing a set of geographical features, based on the JavaScript Object Notation (JSON) standard. It is relatively new, but it has seen a lot of adoption quickly, mostly because it is simpler to create than XML (KML), and JSON has become widely adopted as well for communicating data.

For more detail, see the Wikipedia article for GeoJSON (*http://en.wikipedia.org/wiki/GeoJSON*).

GIS

Geographical information systems (GIS) are systems focused on capturing, managing, and analyzing all sorts of geographical data. It is a broad term, but it is usually used to describe a complete set of tools that handle all aspects of geographical information.

For more detail, see the Wikipedia article for GIS (*http://en.wikipedia.org/wiki/Geographic_information_system*).

KML

> *Keyhole Markup Language* (KML) is an XML standard, as agreed on by the Open Geospatial Consortium, for describing a set of geographical features. It is often used as a "feed," or a machine-readable export of data for a web application.
>
> For more detail, see the Wikipedia article for KML (*http://en.wikipedia.org/wiki/Kml*) and the Wikipedia article for the Open Geospatial Consortium (*http://en.wikipedia.org/wiki/Open_Geospatial_Consortium*), as well as the section "Data Types" on page 17.

Map Tiles

> *Map tiles* or a *tileset* is a collection of digital images of the same size, specifically named for easy retrieval (usually this name incorporates the zoom level and a coordinate system). When the images are put next to each other in the correct order, this creates a complete map for different zoom levels. For instance, a map of the globe at a very low zoom level would only need a few map images to tile together the world (usually four images), but on a very high zoom level, where one could see rooftops, the set of images to make the whole world could be millions.

Raster

> *Raster* data is the idea of storing data as a continuous surface, a grid of pixels. Raster data is most often a digital image or a set of digital images; it can be satellite imagery, or it could be an image of a street map, but the pixels can represent any value. In this format, pixels are used to represent the average of the data that the area the pixel covers.
>
> For more detail, see the Wikipedia article for Raster Data (*http://en.wikipedia.org/wiki/Raster_data*) as well as the section "Data Types" on page 17.

Vector

> A *vector*, specifically a geometric vector, is a geometric entity that has both length (or magnitude) and direction. The direction is the important part that distinguishes one from a scalar value, which is just the magnitude. For geospatial vector data, this is a way of describing where shapes are on the Earth (for instance, the shape of Lake Superior or the location of the closest vegan restaurant).
>
> For more detail, see the Wikipedia subcontent for GIS Vector Data (*http://en.wikipedia.org/wiki/Geographic_information_system#Vector*) as well as the section "Data Types" on page 17.

Web Service

> A *web service* is a broad term used to describe the communication between two applications over the Internet (or any network). For web mapping, this often refers to a web application that provides map tiles or geographical data.
>
> For more detail, see the Wikipedia article for Web Service (*http://en.wikipedia.org/wiki/Web_service*).

WKT

> *Well Known Text* (WKT) is a standard text markup language (a specific way of writing text) for representing vector geometry such as points, lines, and polygons. For instance, a point would be written like this: POINT (30 10). This standard is regulated by the Open Geospatial Consortium.
>
> For more detail, see the Wikipedia article for WKT (*http://en.wikipedia.org/wiki/Well-known_text*) as well as the section "Data Types" on page 17.

Drupal Terms

Drupal is a robust framework and Content Management System (CMS) that provides a specific way of accomplishing tasks. With this system comes a set of terms that may not be obvious to everyone right away. Fortunately, the Drupal community has created an extensive, and growing, list of Drupal glossary terms on Drupal.org (*http://drupal.org/glossary*). The following are some highlighted ones with links that are most relevant to this book:

- block (*http://drupal.org/glossary#block*)
- content type (*http://drupal.org/glossary#content-type*)
- contrib (*http://drupal.org/glossary#contrib*)
- core (*http://drupal.org/glossary#core*)
- entity (*http://drupal.org/glossary#entity*)
- field (*http://drupal.org/glossary#field*)
- issue (*http://drupal.org/glossary#issue*)
- module (*http://drupal.org/glossary#module*)
- node (*http://drupal.org/glossary#node*)
- taxonomy (*http://drupal.org/glossary#taxonomy*)
- theme (*http://drupal.org/glossary#theme*)
- views (*http://drupal.org/glossary#views*)

About the Authors

Alan Palazzolo is a Code for America fellow, and he has been a big contributor to mapping modules, most notably OpenLayers. He maintains several Drupal modules and has been a featured speaker at Drupal events around the world. Alan led the first ever Code Review Sprint to review project applications at DrupalCon Chicago 2011.

Thomas Turnbull has been building websites in PHP since 2002 and working with Drupal since 2006. He has been an organizer for Drupal Camp New York and has been contributor and maintainer for several Drupal modules. He has done Drupal development for Sony Music in New York, where he built sites for artists on their record labels, and he is currently working for Zagat, helping to migrate their website to Drupal.

Get even more for your money.

Join the O'Reilly Community, and register the O'Reilly books you own. It's free, and you'll get:

- $4.99 ebook upgrade offer
- 40% upgrade offer on O'Reilly print books
- Membership discounts on books and events
- Free lifetime updates to ebooks and videos
- Multiple ebook formats, DRM FREE
- Participation in the O'Reilly community
- Newsletters
- Account management
- 100% Satisfaction Guarantee

Signing up is easy:

1. **Go to: oreilly.com/go/register**
2. **Create an O'Reilly login.**
3. **Provide your address.**
4. **Register your books.**

Note: English-language books only

To order books online:
oreilly.com/store

For questions about products or an order:
orders@oreilly.com

To sign up to get topic-specific email announcements and/or news about upcoming books, conferences, special offers, and new technologies:
elists@oreilly.com

For technical questions about book content:
booktech@oreilly.com

To submit new book proposals to our editors:
proposals@oreilly.com

O'Reilly books are available in multiple DRM-free ebook formats. For more information:
oreilly.com/ebooks

O'REILLY®

Spreading the knowledge of innovators   oreilly.com

The information you need, when and where you need it.

With Safari Books Online, you can:

Access the contents of thousands of technology and business books

- Quickly search over 7000 books and certification guides
- Download whole books or chapters in PDF format, at no extra cost, to print or read on the go
- Copy and paste code
- Save up to 35% on O'Reilly print books
- **New!** Access mobile-friendly books directly from cell phones and mobile devices

Stay up-to-date on emerging topics before the books are published

- Get on-demand access to evolving manuscripts.
- Interact directly with authors of upcoming books

Explore thousands of hours of video on technology and design topics

- Learn from expert video tutorials
- Watch and replay recorded conference sessions

Spreading the knowledge of innovators   safari.oreilly.com

Lightning Source UK Ltd.
Milton Keynes UK
UKHW030334050921
389926UK00006B/334